MW01109572

# Miracle in Russia

*Ron & Ginny Cook's*
*Journey in Russian Mission*

Cover design by Kristi Griffith at Thumbprint Creative Arts, GoThumbprint.com.

Layout and editing by Kent Sanders, KentSanders.net.

Scripture quotations are from The Holy Bible, English Standard Version® (ESV®), copyright © 2001 by Crossway, a publishing ministry of Good News Publishers. Used by permission. All rights reserved.

Printed in the United States of America

First printing, 2016

ISBN-10: 1535405473
ISBN-13: 978-1535405478

Mission2Russia.org

*To our brothers and sisters*
*in Kostroma, Russia*
*whom we consider family*

# Contents

# Foreword

THE STORY OF RON AND GINNY'S faithful obedience is remarkable. The events that took place as God led, protected, and overcame are inspiring. God blessed them and the Russian people through their obedience. With equal measure, everyone who reads this book will learn to trust God more and be spurred on in their own ministry.

I was once asked by a Mission to Russia partner, after they had spent a week in Kostroma, Russia, "How would you describe Ron Cook?" Responding was easy. I said, "Ron Cook is hard-wired for ministry and interested in nothing else. He is like a horse wearing blinders, focused and pressing on toward the goal."

That was early in my relationship with Ron. After twenty-three years of partnering with him in ministry, it is still true, but I would add that he is devoted to the Lord and hears his Master's voice. His one desire is to obey no matter the circumstances. He loves people deeply and longs for everyone to know Jesus as Savior. He will selflessly help anyone to accomplish that goal. The same is true of Ginny, as she has faithfully served with and supported Ron in ministry for more than fifty years.

I am so thankful God brought us to minister together. My life has been greatly blessed through their friendship. God has used them to strengthen my faith and show me what it truly means to trust him. I say without hesitation: I have never known anyone more trusting of God than Ron and Ginny Cook.

Thank you, Ron and Ginny, for your unwavering faithful obedience!

Curt Eyman
Mission to Russia Board Member

# Prologue

OUR PURPOSE IN GOING TO Russia was simple. We were going to start a church and bring her to maturity in Christ through biblical teaching. We believed it would be best to create a Russian church, not an American missionary church.

This book details God's work through our journey to preach the gospel in a foreign, godless country. It is not about our great feats and accomplishments. We cannot be given credit for the amazing things that happened along this journey. God was in charge every step of the way. In truth, most things were accomplished despite our lack of "missionary preparedness."

Many godly people decide to become missionaries and seek a mission field in which to minister. Sometimes people become missionaries after hearing the inspiring stories of others who have left the comfort of home to serve a people group different from themselves. Nothing is wrong with that. But our story begins in a different way.

God pursued us. We were not looking to enter the mission field. We had no idea that there was an opportunity in Russia and probably wouldn't have pursued the opportunity even if we had known about it.

It seemed that God had a hand in every area of our life: in preparing our hearts, overcoming nearly impossible obstacles in the preparations after our initial decision to go, and leading us into the work ahead of us. He opened doors, pushed us through, and got His work done in spite of our lack of correct planning. We cannot take any of the glory for what God has done. He is the one who opened our eyes to this need and filled our lives with His grace and blessings.

# Introduction

A MIRACLE IS AN EFFECT of extraordinary events in the physical world that surpasses all known human or natural powers and is ascribed to a supernatural cause. Through the pages of this book, our hope is that you will see the miracles God performed throughout our mission in Russia. We pray that our stories will move you to know, follow, and trust Him like never before.

The following account of our missionary journey meets all of the qualifications of the definition above. The only explanation for any success we achieved in our ministry is God himself. This publication lays out how God worked in our ministry from May 1992 through our last goodbyes in June 2015.

# Chapter 1

## *The Harvest is Plentiful*

GROWING UP IN THE 1950S and 60s in America, I was raised to think of Russia as the enemy. According to the news outlets, problems and threats between the United States and Russia were prevalent. We continually heard about the Cold War causing friction between the States and Russia. Throughout the 70s, 80s, and even the 90s, the cultural attitude, and thus my own, hardly changed. I considered Russia and its people, as Ronald Reagan referred to them, to be an "evil empire."

In 1992, I was preaching at Valley Center Christian Church in Kansas, when a church member came to me and asked if I would be interested in taking a mission trip to Russia. The Soviet Union had fallen in 1990, meaning doorways for the gospel were now wide open. Instinctively, I gave it zero thought and said I was not interested. I couldn't even consider the idea of going to Russia. It was the furthest thing from my mind. But she would not give up. She asked and poked and prodded, until out of desperation, I agreed to go with her group to Russia, but I gave one condition. My wife, Ginny, and I would go only if we were able to raise enough money for us both to go. This was my clever plan to say yes, and yet not have to go. There was no way to raise enough money in such a short time, and there was no way we would be going. I was sure of it.

It wasn't that I was against short-term mission trips. I had taken part in short-term mission work before. But this was Russia! Our enemy! It was so ingrained in me to think of Russia in this way.

As you could have guessed, though, I was shocked to find that funds were successfully raised to send both of us on the trip. Thus, I was completely out of excuses. This trip was going to happen. We weren't angry, but we certainly weren't excited. Looking back now, we can see clearly how God orchestrated these events. There was a divine plan underway. Ginny and I had no idea our lives were about to change in a radical way.

*St. Basil's Cathedral, Moscow (1992)*

We landed in Moscow and found ourselves in the midst of mass confusion as we navigated through the airport and went through long lines at the visa checkpoint. We were then herded into busses that took us to a motel. We were traveling with a large team set up by the Revival Fires ministry. Ginny and I didn't know what we were going to be doing. We found ourselves in a group of about seven people heading to the city of Kostroma. We had never heard of Kostroma, but we were told it was about 250 miles northeast of Moscow. So, in late May of 1992, we found ourselves in this city of 250,000 people along the Volga River—the city that, unbeknownst to us, would soon become our home.

Our group passed out thousands of Bibles on the streets of Kostroma, and a theater had been rented for five nights of evangelistic meetings. We also held evangelistic meetings at a college, in orphanages, and in schools. The meetings went well. Crowds upon crowds of people packed into the buildings. There were many baptisms in just two weeks. The people of Kostroma were starving for a message of hope, something that they hadn't heard throughout more than seventy years of godless Communist rule.

When the time came to return to America, Ginny left with the group, but I felt led to stay behind. The opportunity to share the gospel was astounding at that time in Russia. The harvest was plentiful, but the workers were few (Matthew 9:37). Dozens of American Christians were going on short-term trips to Russia, but it appeared that no one had any plans to stick around, disciple believers, or establish churches. I investigated as much as possible for three weeks. Not knowing the language, I required an interpreter to travel with me everywhere. I held meetings every night in the same theater the Revival Fires ministry had rented. During the day, I went all over town asking questions, trying to find out if anyone had a long term plan for ministry in Kostroma.

My extra time in Kostroma made two things evident. First was the great need for someone to stay and teach these new Christians. There was a great void in the area of discipleship. It would be so difficult for these new believers to know how to grow in their faith without someone to help them along the way. They had no one to show them what it means to follow Jesus. Second, the Lord was convicting me personally to bring Christ to this city. I felt a strong calling, and yet I really struggled with it. I had been raised to believe that I was in enemy country. The prejudice was hardwired in me, let alone the fact that I didn't know the language, and I didn't understand anything about the country or its customs.

When the time came to fly back to the States, I spent the duration of the flight thinking through this calling I was feeling. Honestly, I was kind of a mess. I was on the verge of breaking down all nine hours on the plane. I knew what God was calling me to do, yet I argued every way that I could, "Lord, I don't know the language. I don't know the culture. They won't accept me. They consider me their enemy. I haven't had any missionary training. I already have a ministry that I enjoy." These hesitations weighed on me, but the one that weighed the most was "How could I ask Ginny to live in Kostroma, a city which had a standard of living equal to that of a third world country?"

As the plane was landing, I felt a calm come over me. I knew in my heart that God would take care of us if we chose to follow His plan for us. Ginny met me at the airport, and for a while we traveled in silence. Neither one of us knew exactly how to start or what to say. Once we started talking, it became evident that she had felt this calling just as I had. Anxious as we were, we knew that it was God leading us. He had planted a seed in us, a passion for these people. This confirmation took away our biggest fear—that one of us didn't feel this calling.

As it turns out, deciding to go was easy compared to the work to be done to actually get there. We owned a house, two cars, and furniture. We were in debt and needed to raise a significant amount of support to make this work. We knew we couldn't do it on our own, so we put our trust in God and asked for help from others.

We began by talking to our church leadership. After some thought and prayer, they said they would be happy to support us. During the next six months, we put our house up for sale, as well as our cars and furniture, and began raising support. Keep in mind that we were in our 50s when we decided to start a new chapter of life in a foreign country. Human as we are, our thoughts were overflowing with questions, doubts, and fears. In moments of weakness, we doubted ourselves and doubted God's plan for us. He reaffirmed our decision over and over. The best example of this was a letter Ginny received from Inga, a college student in Kostroma.

Ginny had met a few young ladies, Inga included, who were studying English at the local university. She spent a lot of time with them discussing the basics of Christianity—God, Jesus, the Bible, and what those things meant for them. We rejoiced when a couple of these ladies accepted Christ, but Inga was not one of them. As we were contemplating our move to Russia, we received this letter from Inga. When this letter arrived from over 6,000 miles away, we were intrigued, to say the least. As Ginny opened the handwritten letter and began to read, tears welled up in her eyes. She cried as she read it to me.

*Dear Ginny,*

*How are you? I'm missing you, Ginny. It was so pleasant to talk to you. I wish we continued our conversation, but unfortunately you had to return to America so soon. But I think we'll talk in our letters. Do you want?*

*Ginny, you know my parents don't want me to become a Christian. I don't mean that they don't allow me to be a Christian, but they say that our religions are very different, there's nothing wrong if I'll become a Christian (as they say) but when all Americans leave our town, we who want to be a Christian, or have already become will be alone here, there will be not our church. My mother is afraid that one day we'll have a lot of enemies and we'll have no strength to fight, for there'll be very few of us. In a word, she says a lot of things, Ginny. I don't know what is right. I'm at a loss. Please help me, Ginny. I'm waiting for your letter!*

*With Love,*
*Inga*

Upon hearing Inga's letter, I found that I was also in tears. Our hearts broke for these people who were hungry for God's love. We felt the burden heavily on us that if not us, who would go and minister to them? Inga's letter confirmed without a doubt that we were making the right decision. This letter served to strengthen our faith and give us courage when we needed it most.

In a short time, our home, cars, and furniture sold. This allowed us to get out of debt, and we raised all the necessary support in only five months. We have always known it was God's intervention alone that caused this to happen so quickly. That in itself was miraculous. God did not have to bless us with such a smooth transition, but He did so out of His great love for us and for His people in Russia.

As we prepared to go, we felt we needed a name for this ministry, a way to let people know who we were and what our purpose was. After some prayer and consideration, we became Mission to Russia. It was simple, but it was clear and true. God had given us a mission, and it was in Russia! Our purpose in going to Russia was simply this: to start a church and teach her to maturity. It was important to us that the church would become a Russian church, not an American missionary-led church in Russia.

As we look back now, we can only laugh at how much God accomplished in spite of our lack of missionary preparedness. Back then, we didn't know how most missionaries would go about preparing for cross-cultural missions. We later understood that a typical missionary-in-training would scope out a certain country they might like to work in. Then, they would visit the country and possibly meet with a specific organization already working there.

Next, after deciding on a country, they would begin the process by sharing their plan with their home church, family and friends, to raise awareness and support. Some would choose to take a year or two of language courses, as well as investigate the cultural climate of the land they intended to go to. They would raise funds not only for the mission work and their salary, but also for retirement. All these things would typically be achieved through a missionary sending agency who would keep their records, do their taxes, and send them funds on a regular basis.

After this, a typical missionary-in-training would go on a short-term trip to work with a mission to gain experience. This would be invaluable experience, preparing them for what it is like to assimilate into a new culture and for married couples to live out what it's like to support one another in a new dynamic in a foreign land.

Purely out of ignorance, Ginny and I did not follow any guidelines like what other missionaries would consider as enough preparation for mission work. When we recognized God's calling, we simply set out to go. We were certain God wanted us in the city of Kostroma, and we hoped to finish preparations and arrive there in six months' time. We raised support, got out of debt, and at the age of 50, set out to a new land. We felt how we imagine Abraham and Sarah felt, advanced in years and just trusting God.

We did not study the language or culture. We didn't visit Russia a second time before deciding. We did not go through a mission-sending agency or have another person or family going with us. We did not plan for retirement or have a fallback plan in case we were sent back to the States, which was very possible, and actually happened to us later on.

We had no idea how much money it would take to live in Kostroma. We took what we hoped would be enough money to rent an apartment and purchase food and ministry supplies for three months. Then, a set amount would be sent each quarter by someone stateside. We weren't sure how the money would get to us or how much money would actually reach us because Russian banks at that time were rather untrustworthy. We hadn't even looked for a place to live before we arrived.

I would not recommend this as a way to start a mission work. We simply did not know about all the preparations that could have helped us. Language studies in particular would have been a great help. Perhaps we did things just as God intended.

With the peace of knowing that our friends were praying for us, we left for Russia. In a worldly sense, we were set up for failure, and if we were on our own, I'm certain we would have failed. But this plan didn't originate with us. It was God's plan. He opened so many doors, and we just went through them. He protected us, likely in ways that we don't even know about. He made sure we received our financial support each quarter so that we could continue in the work He had for us. There was always just enough, barely, but always precisely what we needed.

## *Harder Than We Thought*

November 1992 marks the beginning of many obstacles and trials, but also some of the greatest of God's blessings we have ever known. We traveled to Kostroma, again with the Revival Fires team, and worked with them in the same theater. Ginny and I were overflowing with excitement and anticipation seeing so many lost souls accept Christ during the revival week. But this time, as the team left, we stayed behind, and it got real incredibly fast. The doubt and fear crept back in, and on top of that we quickly became lonely. We were alone in Russia.

We were left out in the country where the American team had stayed in Kozlovy Gory, roughly seven miles from Kostroma. It was the middle of winter, and there was snow everywhere, up to four feet deep. We had no phone, not that we could have used it as the operator spoke only Russian. All we had with us were a few suitcases of clothes, books, children's ministry materials, and an electric keyboard. I had recently slipped on a marble staircase and broken my wrist. Ginny was ill. Trying to communicate with the doctor was quite an experience as they couldn't speak English, and we couldn't speak Russian. Ginny held her stomach, put her hand in her mouth and pretended she was throwing up—her way of trying to tell the doctor her symptoms. It was like medical charades. She was diagnosed with food poisoning, and recovered after hesitantly taking some medicine the doctor gave her. We had no food to eat. We couldn't really talk to anyone. We felt overwhelmed.

FROM MY WIFE, GINNY:

*The Americans we had been with flew back to America, and we returned to Kostroma in two cars. We rode in one car and the other contained all of our luggage. Uri Duroff, a Russian helper to Revival Fires, and his son Sergey were in charge of getting us back to Kostroma. We left Moscow at 12:00 and arrived at our destination at 8:00. It took eight hours to travel 250 miles.*

*We had no hot water and very little heat. This place was a summer house where the military would come for rest. It was a beautiful place full of suites with high ceilings and velvet drapery. It was nice but now it was past the season for use and was basically closed, so we were allowed only a tiny bit of heat.*

*The few people we knew were helping us look for a place to live, but housing was scarce because of the military returning home following the fall of Communism. Inflation was taking its toll and prices were much higher, almost double from six months earlier, but we knew the Lord would supply the right place in his own timing.*

*One big lesson we were learning right away was that it's*

*best not to plan too thoroughly in Russia. Oh, you can plan, just allow for the plans to unravel at any moment. Of course, this happens occasionally in America, but I would say it is much more often the case in Russia.*

To say we were down in the dumps was an understatement. We were holed up in a room for a few days with little heat and little to eat when a knock came on our door. Standing at the door was a young man maybe thirteen years old with his arms full. He didn't speak English, but it became clear that he wanted to feed us. He had brought food from the town. He had approached the people running the facility where we were staying, and they had allowed him to cook us a meal. As soon as he gave us the food, he left. Then, we realized we had recognized him. He had helped the American team unload the material for the revivals. But how he knew where we were or that we needed food is something that only God knows. It may seem small, but we felt so blessed by his generosity.

From our first trip in May, we knew three English students who had worked as interpreters during the Revival Fires campaign. It took some time to track them down and reconnect with them. Thankfully, they were interested in helping us and so they did, more so on Sundays because they were in college during the week. The five of us were able get things rolling. It meant a lot to have even a few people supporting us and who spoke some English. One of the students had a brother-in-law who spoke English well enough and would help us throughout the week while the ladies were in school.

GINNY:

*Seven days after arriving in Kostroma, we were losing weight quickly, yet we were upbeat and excited. The property owner, Lena, came to our door. She was concerned that I might become sick, so she moved us to a smaller house that was warmer. It was a small thing, but it was huge to us.*

*The next day, we were taken to a place where we could eat decent meals for very little money. It was a cafeteria in the basement of the City Administration building. We were allowed to eat lunch there with our interpreter each weekday. Most days, this was our only full size meal. God was taking care of us in so many ways.*

*One day, a couple of ladies who worked on the property in which we lived, brought us some groceries: a bag of potatoes, onions, bread, and some butter. Unfortunately, we had no way to cook them. So, the ladies brought us an electric burner, a pan, and a few dishes. They were so generous. It filled our hearts.*

# Russia's Religious Background

We would find that one of the greatest obstacles in our ministry was not the "evil" Russian government. To our surprise it turned out to be the Russian Orthodox Church.

To give you some background, the Russian Orthodox Church is a by-product of the Greek Orthodox Church, which split from the Roman Catholic Church. In the 900s, a Russian leader named Vladimir went to Constantinople, the head of the Greek church, and brought the components of the church back to Russia and it became the official church of Russia. Some of those components included style of worship, the onion top roof style of the buildings, icon paintings, worship of Mary, and so on.

The church went through many battles during the next several hundred years, from outside influences, to inside takeovers, to government takeovers. Tzars (tyrannical leaders) ruled the church in the years leading up to the revolution of 1917, and they basically ruled Russia as well. This made way for the revolution because of the extreme poverty forced upon people. The church spent millions of rubles building hundreds of unnecessary churches with their gold-painted onion tops, massive architecture, and icon paintings, all while their people were starving.

*Church of the Resurrection, an Orthodox church in Kostroma, Russia*

The political weakness of the country, along with the people's dislike of the tzars, allowed a fairly easy takeover by Communist and atheistic leader Vladimir Lenin. Lenin's first action of his new regime was to rid the country of religion, which he believed to be the cause of Russia's demise. He destroyed most of the church buildings and disposed of church leaders by either killing them or sending them to Siberia. He left just enough church buildings to make it appear as though the country still had religion, but he placed KGB agents in them who posed as "priests" so that any confessions made by the people would be reported back to the government, and the people would be punished.

So from 1925 to 1990, under the regimes of Vladimir Lenin, Joseph Stalin, and Nikita Khrushchev, Russia was for all intents and purposes without religion, without faith. Two whole generations grew up not knowing about God. During this time, they were without Bibles because the Bible was outlawed. When Communism fell in 1990, the government was in disarray. Everything was up in the air, complete chaos.

It was at this time that the Orthodox church reawakened, and the priests attempted to put the pieces of the church back to its original state. In trying to regain the confidence of the people, they became part of the new government and became the state church. They desired to control the people, to get them back in church. Not just any church, but Orthodox churches only. They saw outsiders, like us, influencing the people for other denominations and felt threatened. They tried frantically to get rid of those influences. There were literally hundreds of different religions, churches, and cults pouring into Russia after the fall of Communism. The Russian Orthodox Church had no tolerance for any of these new beliefs and considered them all enemies of the church.

This was the atmosphere we found ourselves in when we started our church in Kostroma. The Orthodox church was working tirelessly to get all foreigners out. They threatened their own people, instructing them to stay away from "infidel" churches or else they would lose their burial rights. There was even a full-page story in the largest Moscow paper telling lies about Ginny and me and our church. They were creative in their attempts to knock us down. However, if you suffer as a Christian, do not be ashamed, but praise God that you bear that name (1 Peter 4:16).

The Russian Orthodox Church taught, and still teaches, chiefly about God's judgment, and how disobedience would send them to hell. They do not speak of God's love and forgiveness. Their idea of obedience is obeying the patriarchal head of the local church as well as its traditions and rules, rather than what the Bible teaches. The Orthodox church believes in infant baptism, and would baptize every baby that was born if they could—essentially causing every Russian to grow up as a Russian Orthodox Christian without a choice. That is just another reason why it was, and still is, difficult to work with the Orthodox churches. The Russian people were told that they were already Christians. As a result, so many people saw no need to be part of another Christian movement, especially one that was led by foreigners.

For some people, however, it was this very belief system that led them to seek something more. They heard about our church, and when they came they heard about a God who loved them, as opposed to a God who wished to punish their every wrong move. Many people would hear the good news of Jesus and leap into it in faith, wanting to learn more and have a relationship with a loving, forgiving God.

## *Settling In*

GINNY:

*We had been in Russia for five weeks, when one morning Sergey came by with a newspaper ad for a three-room flat to rent. We went to the flat owner's house and waited in the car while Bob and Sergey conducted business. They always wanted to take care of business for us because we are American and they felt they must protect us. They offered the landlord $75 US dollars a month. It was a new unit, never lived in, and in a good part of town. Our offer was accepted, and we prepared to move in.*

*When renting a flat in Kostroma you receive it bare—one porcelain sink and stove in the kitchen and in the bathroom a tub, sink, and toilet. No light fixtures, drapes, cabinets, or any kind of furniture. So we spent the next few days preparing to make it livable. Ron and Sergey spent every day going all over town looking for pieces of furniture. We had next to no choices,* and were happy to find anything. It was an adventure collecting piece by piece.

We had moved into the flat a week before Christmas. Until then, we were not aware that Russians didn't celebrate Christmas on December 25th. Sergey informed us that they celebrated on January 7. But we were so new to Russia, and felt in our hearts that we wanted to celebrate on December 25th.

I decided to attempt a nice roast dinner and invite two of our young interpreters, Sergey and Alex, to join us for lunch. This was no easy task as the stove was subject to surges in heat and at other times to lack heat. I was told to lay a brick in the bottom to absorb the extra heat, but it didn't make a huge difference. I did manage to get the food I needed and even baked apple crisp for dessert as I had brought brown sugar with us from America. It wasn't available in Russia.

So the guys came and just as we were sitting down to eat, a lady and her daughter, Tatiana and Cindy, stopped by. They wanted us to know that they were thinking about us today as we were so far away from family. So they joined us for the meal.

After dinner, the doorbell rang again. Bob and Sergey brought us a Christmas tree that they had cut down themselves. Along with them were six other people. I quickly tried to think of something we could do. I got out some construction paper so we could make colored rings to drape on the tree. I also had some chewing gum, and we made ornaments out of the foil wrappers. I was so touched by this house full of generous people that I wanted to show them my gratitude. A lightbulb went off *in my head remembering we had a couple of trunks of used clothing that had been given to us at the last moment, and we had brought them with us. They were filled with jeans, sweaters, shirts, etc. We got them out and told everyone to take a couple of things that they could wear or use.*

*Oh, I wish you could have seen their faces. They were so excited and they looked through each piece and decided who it would fit until everyone had a gift. I went to bed that night feeling that this day had been one of the best Christmases in my entire life. God is so good.*

We went into it with a plan in mind, steps we would take to start a church. Unfortunately, due to the cultural situation and day-to-day circumstances, we had to ditch our plan and start from scratch.

So, the new plan was basically prayer. We knelt before God daily, and we held fast to hope that He would reveal His plan. We were able to rent the same theater that we had used during the revivals. We occupied the theater for three hours on Sunday mornings. To inform the community, we ran an ad in the newspaper about services being held by an American preacher. Unable to do much on our own, we were learning to lean on our young interpreters as they had better connections and were able to make more arrangements than we could manage. We didn't know them very well, but we had to trust them. We didn't have much of a choice, so we simply had to trust.

As we look back, we know that God had a hand in picking them out. There is no telling what could have happened with dishonest people. We could easily have been taken advantage of or mistreated.

## Sunday Services

Our first Sunday morning service was truly amazing. There was a snowstorm in the middle of the night, and the snow was up to four feet deep everywhere. When we woke up, we thought there was no way anyone would leave the comfort of their home to attend a church service in this type of weather. As we got closer to the theater, we didn't see a soul or a car in sight, so we were not expecting to even have the service. Upon entering the theater, we were dumbfounded to see that the theater was overflowing with people. You could barely get through the aisles.

GINNY:

*Approaching our first Sunday service, I felt so ill prepared and wondered how Ron and I would do what normally a team of 4-7 people would do. Our transportation arrived late (surprise!) which made us late to the theater. It was a very cold -30*

*Children's Theater, first location of Kostroma Christian Church*

*degrees celsius (-22 fahrenheit)! Somehow, the colder the weather, the greater attendance we had—guess they couldn't do anything else. We had over 340 people in our first service, though the hall had seating for only 175. They just crammed in everywhere with most adults holding children on their laps. Many, Ron and me included, stood for the whole service, which was an hour and a half long. I gave a lesson with the flannel graph and sang a solo. Ron preached, then we served communion. Following that service we had ten baptisms!*

God was working in the lives of the Russian people in such a way as I had never seen in my thirty years of ministry in the States. There were baptisms every Sunday, sometimes as many as twenty-five baptisms in one service! Every week people responded during the invitation hymn. We will always remember one Sunday when all of our interpreters accepted

Christ and were baptized, including Inga, the student who wrote the letter to Ginny.

A prison ministry in Moscow had blessed us with a baptistery. We carried the portable fiberglass baptistery by bus to Kostroma. Using buckets we would fill the tub with water, and then when we were done with it, we had to bucket the water back out. We did this every Sunday for five years. Today, that same baptistery is still being used in the church in Kostroma. It has been permanently installed with running water and a drain.

The Sunday morning services were going great, but there had to be more to the ministry than just two or three hours of singing and preaching on Sunday morning. Hundreds of people came to the theater to see "the Americans" and to get one of the free Bibles we handed out, but they had no interest in coming a second time. We had no way of keeping track of all these people with foreign names, and no one was willing to give us their address.

We wanted to do more than Sunday services, so we decided to try a ministry for children. Ginny started an after-school children's ministry that met at the theater. Unfortunately, due to the country's instability, most parents weren't willing to leave their children with strangers from America, so that didn't work out.

GINNY:

*One evening, we had unexpected company at our suite—Sergey and two of his friends. I was not prepared for company. I felt the need to offer them food, but we didn't really have much. I dug through our suitcases and found some packs of instant soup and some instant hot chocolate. We topped if off with some granola bars. It felt good to share our meager supply when so many had been generous to us.*

*The next day Bob picked us up in a car and took us to meet the director of the children's center. Kostroma had recently become a sister city to Durham, North Carolina, and so this center had interactions with that city, and they wanted to speak to us. By the time we were done talking I had agreed to teach English to the children at the center. I would teach two classes three times a week, and I would also offer piano lessons. Ron would be teaching English to adults plus an advanced English course to high school students.*

*We found this to be a great opportunity to serve. We asked if we could teach Christian ethics along with the lessons, and the director agreed. He was concerned about how much they could pay us. When we said we were prepared to do it for nothing, he was astounded. We told him to just make it known that this was our gift to the people of Kostroma. We later found out that the director was on the city council and could help us in other ways. Making contacts was invaluable. We needed all the help we could get.*

## *An Incredibly Unique Opportunity*

After we had been in Kostroma a couple of months, one of our interpreters shared with us that a public school teacher wanted us to come and teach a Bible class in their school! We were floored. Even in America one couldn't just go share the gospel in a public school.

It was surreal. We knew we had no choice but to say yes and get ready to go to the school to teach the Bible! We were given some guidelines. They wanted us to teach on six different accounts from the Bible beginning with the creation in Genesis and ending with the death, burial, and resurrection of Jesus. Uh, yeah, we can do that! We had brought from America a set of the large flannel graph backdrops and figures to teach almost every story in the Bible (they look the same in all languages), so this was a key element of teaching these lessons.

They were quite a hit. Many other schools started calling us, asking for the people with the large picture Bible stories. Soon we were teaching 8-10 times a week in the schools. Looking back now, we realized this was a big part of the foundation of the Kostroma church. Many of the children we taught in the public schools later brought their parents to church when we began offering Sunday School classes.

*Ron & Ginny Cook in Kostroma, Russia (1993)*

GINNY:

*Because the Russian children were so artistic and enjoyed doing crafts, I made sure this was a big part of my lessons. It was challenging for me, as I am not very crafty or artsy. Thankfully, it didn't take much to please the kids.*

*In those days, not many craft supplies were available in Kostroma. I always brought everything from the U.S. I would fill three or four suitcases with crayons, scissors, glue, colored paper, pencils, markers, paper plates, stickers, and more. I did this about every 12-18 months. Our friends stateside supported this effort in a big way. Even if it was just leftovers from a VBS, it helped.*

*We were invited into several schools over a matter of months. Often the teachers would combine their classes, and I would teach two classes for 90 minutes at a time. We often had 70-80 students in these groups. Sometimes it was a one-time deal, and other times it led to 6-8 weeks of teaching. I always*

*taught the creation story and the fall of man first. The students'
reactions always amazed me. They accepted it so openly. Many
said that it answered questions that they had always had. We
gave out copies of the New Testament plus Psalms to each child.*

*These were busy times, but great times, as I was preparing
and teaching up to fourteen lessons a week. We were also spending time teaching in an orphanage until again the Orthodox
Church stepped in and stopped it, saying they were taking over
the religious instruction at the orphanage. One school asked if I
could teach Bible lessons after school dismissed to children who
were waiting for their parents to get off work. We were able to
teach in public schools for over two years. So much teaching—so
many seeds planted!*

*When summer came, we were invited to an English sum-
mer camp program two days a week to teach Bible lessons. We
taught two classes each day, one for those 12 years of age and
under, then for those over 12. We had such a great time with
these kids. Several were baptized in the river that ran near the
camp. Then a dance summer camp wanted in on the action, so
we did the same for them. With both camps, students and
teachers, we taught over 1200 people that summer. We were
experiencing God's miracles all around us and were so blessed
to be a part of it.*

*Igor and his family*

# *Igor*

One day after Ginny told the story with the flannel graph to a group of public school kids, as the children were working on a color and cut worksheet, I noticed a tiny little boy with a sad look on his face sitting on the front row doing nothing. I went over to him to see if he needed help, and when I got closer I noticed that his fingers were sort of webbed together. I gently took one of his hands, placed a crayon in it, and helped him color the picture. Then I helped him cut it out and glue it where it went. He had such a wide smile on his face when we were finished.

We found out his name was Igor and that he had a rare disease. From what I understood, he was born with only one layer of skin. (The average person has three layers of skin.) This left him susceptible to sores all over his body that took a long time to heal, and he was also susceptible to infections that affected internal parts of his body. He was small for his age, very thin. Sadly, he was an outcast. His teachers didn't take time to teach him or help him physically or mentally. The other school children were mean to him and called him names.

We were able to go to Igor's class once a week for two years, and every time he was so joyful as we would help him with his worksheets. He would listen so intently to the Bible stories. We finally met his mother one day. She told us that Igor had brought home every picture he had colored in our class and posted them on the walls of his bedroom. She and the boy's sister had learned about Jesus from those pictures. We learned from his mother, who was a nurse, that Igor was not given much time to live because of the infections that came with the sores all over his body. She was preparing herself for Igor's death, which could come at any time. But for the first time in her life she also saw hope in Jesus.

GINNY:

*I loved children's ministry, and had 30 years of experience before coming to Russia. I was also eager to minister to women. I noticed that women seemed to do a lot of work—washing clothes by hand, raising children, cooking, and cleaning—but they seemed to have no joy in their lives. I invited women to join me on Tuesday mornings for Bible study and prayer. This was my first time teaching women, but it was delightful. They soaked up everything we studied like sponges. They loved learning about God and getting to know each other. They began to trust each other. I think not trusting each other was within them from living under Communist rule.*

*One morning, as we were meeting, one lady asked what we should do with all the beggars on the streets asking for money for food, who usually ended up buying alcohol. We made a plan to carry around food bags, bread and cheese, so when a beggar reached out, we could offer to pray for them and offer them some food. They were not hearers of the word only, but also doers (James 1:22).*

## House of Nature

We were eventually pushed out of the theater when they started showing movies earlier and earlier, despite our agreement with them. We suspect it was

*House of Nature, the second location of the church*

because the government was discouraging businesses from working with foreign missionaries. It took some time to find a new location, but God was preparing a place for us. He brought us to a place known as the House of Nature, which was home to animals like lizards, snakes, fish, and also plants. Many classes took field trips there. It was located in a two-story building, but the House of Nature only utilized the first floor, leaving the top floor open to us.

It was perfect for what we needed at that time because there was a big meeting room we could use for Sunday services and a few smaller rooms for classes, small groups, and office space. The large room seated about 250 people. An added bonus was that the room even had a piano.

Since we now had an address, we had to file paperwork with the government to make us a "legal" church. To our amazement, we were granted the right to call ourselves a church. Despite being pushed out of the theater, we were now legally "Kostroma Christian Church." We recognized that God definitely had a hand in this, and we praised Him for it!

We hit the ground running with Sunday school classes, inviting children from all the schools we had been in. We also invited anyone and everyone we met on the streets. In a short time, our classrooms were overflowing. Ginny quickly began teaching a few volunteers how to teach Sunday school, and the church grew rapidly.

It was in this building that Igor started bringing his mom and sister to Sunday school classes, and it was not long before Igor wanted to be baptized. By now, he had heard many stories from the Bible, and he knew what the Bible taught about baptism. I had a long talk with Igor because there was an issue with his decision to be baptized. It wasn't that he didn't understand or wasn't old enough. Rather, the problem was with the sores all over his body. I warned him that if we baptized him, it would aggravate the open sores and cause him pain. This did not deter him. He was determined to be baptized. He was ready, and his mother approved of his decision.

As he stepped into the water, you could hear a little whimper from his lips. He was lowered into the water and when he came up out of the water, he let out a blood-curdling scream that could be heard all over the building. Once he was dressed in dry clothes, he immediately went around the room telling everyone that they needed Jesus, that they needed to be baptized.

Our church was a safe, loving place for Igor. He found acceptance and friendship in the church, as his brothers and sisters in Christ loved him for who he was. A short time later, his mother and sister were also baptized. All this started from hanging up those Bible pictures he had colored in school. God used Igor to touch the lives of many.

I cannot conclude this story without jumping forward about four years. Igor was now 14 years old. He had already lived much longer than the doctors expected. Even so, he had gone through several blood transfusions and was beginning to decline. We were preparing to make a trip back to the States to renew our visas and visit our supporting churches when I received a call that Igor wanted to see me.

I went to his apartment, and there he was in his bed, so small. I hadn't seen him for a while, and his condition was startling. He barely had any strength to talk, but I prayed over him and then I saw his little finger waving for me to come closer to him. Both the interpreter and I drew in close as he whispered "Thank you. I'm praying for you." I could no longer hold back my tears. In his condition, he was praying for me. We left him with heavy hearts knowing he would likely be gone before we returned from our visit to the States.

During our trip, we indeed got word that Igor had passed away. We mourned the loss of a special boy who profoundly impacted our church. And we rejoiced in the fact that we will one day see Igor in Heaven, flawless and uninhibited by earthly imperfections.

# Chapter 2

## *Chaotic Times in Russia*

THE ORTHODOX CHURCH WAS NOT the only obstacle in sharing Jesus with the people of Russia. God worked despite the economic and political situation to open doors for the gospel to be preached in Kostroma. We first traveled to Russia right after Perestroika, a political movement for reformation within the Communist Party of the Soviet Union during the 1980s, when everything had collapsed. The economic system was in total disorder. The political mindset of the population was "every man for himself." They knew they wanted the freedom to make their own decisions, yet they didn't know what decisions to make. This was a foreign idea to them.

The ruble, Russia's currency, was losing value

each day. When we moved to Russia, the exchange rate was 120 rubles to one dollar. At the end of our first year, it was 500 to one, and by the second year it was in the thousands to one. This was beneficial to us, because as the ruble lost value, the U.S. dollar had more purchasing power in Russia. The more the ruble fell, the less we paid for the apartment in American dollars. This made a huge difference for us. As much as it benefited us, it was devastating for the Russian people. Not only was their purchasing power decreasing, but their inflation was drastically rising. Some items remained inexpensive because the government held the necessities like milk, bread, and eggs at a low price, but any and all nonessentials were insanely expensive.

GINNY:

*Buying groceries was an experience. I made a list: salt, pepper, sugar, milk, eggs, dishwashing soap, and a plastic bucket. Sounded easy enough. Bob, our daytime helper, and Sergey, our driver, took us to the store. It turned out there was no salt or sugar available at this time. You had to have a sugar card and a salt card from the city administration in order to purchase those items. We managed to get some eggs, but little did I know that they just hand you as many eggs as you want with no carton of any kind. I couldn't find pepper, but I did get a bottle of milk, dish soap, and a bucket.*

*Shopping for food was always an adventure. We would often go to several places before we could find even simple items like flour or oats. The store had most things in gunny sacks so I always needed to take along bags for them to fill and weigh the merchandise. I had to take jars if I wanted sour cream or ketchup. We spent a lot of time waiting in lines hoping to get butter or cheese, only to have it run out just before we got to the front of the line. But the bread, oh the bread! We bought it at the bakery or sometimes off a bread truck that drove around the city. The bread was always warm and fresh. We usually bought two loaves—one to take home and one to eat on the way.*

*One morning, early on in our time in Russia, I had returned home from grocery shopping to find the elevator out of order. By the time I reached our flat, I was exhausted, both physically and mentally. I sat everything down and sank to the floor. Tears flowing, I said aloud, "Lord, how much longer must I do this?" After a good cry, I got up, put things away, and carried on.*

*About ten hours later, the phone rang. My sister was calling. It was the middle of the night in Russia, and international calls were running four dollars per minute, so we tried to keep it brief. She asked me if something was wrong. I said, "No, I don't think so." She asked again, sharing that a couple from her church had contacted her. They had each individually felt led to pray for me and wanted to know if there was anything specific they should pray for.*

*I was astounded. I didn't know that couple, had never met them, and yet they were called to pray for me. My sister and I realized that they began praying for me just as I was sinking to the floor. God has His eyes on His children. I fully learned this truth that day: He cares deeply about even our smallest hurts.*

The economy only declined further when employment rates sank. A multitude of citizens lost their jobs due to factories closing. The equipment was worn out and needed replaced, but repairs or replacements simply weren't possible. For most people, the new jobs they found didn't pay enough to feed them and their families. The average wage at the time was $50 a month, and the unemployment rate was at 50%. Goods could not be manufactured fast enough to keep up.

Bread was cheap, about five cents a loaf, but you had to stand in long lines to buy it. Most stores, including pharmacies, had empty shelves and didn't know when they would receive any new products. Finding enough food to eat each day was hard work. The streets and highways were in terrible shape with huge holes and no plans or funds to repair them. There was a 13-year waiting period to get a phone in one's home, and the Kostroma telephone phone system had not been upgraded since it was installed in 1907.

Only about 10% of people in Kostroma had a car. Everyone else depended on busses, trolley busses, and trains to get around. However, these too were breaking down and not being repaired. Crime and suicide rates were on the rise throughout the country. The people of Russia were truly hurting. Depression and a general lack of zeal for life was evident across the entire country.

The darker it is, the brighter a light shines. People were desperate for something to bring joy into their lives. When we would baptize and disciple people, there was a clear difference in the way they carried themselves. They had something to believe in, a hope for the future, a God who loved them and cared about them. You could see the joy on their faces in comparison with the rest of the population. Others noticed and would ask them what changed. We were not afraid to tell them the good news of Jesus. In the first five years of our ministry, more than 1,000 people received Jesus as Savior and were baptized. We were able to see clearly God's purpose for sending us to this city at this particular time in history!

# Partners in Ministry

God opened many doors of ministry in those first two years. We were involved in prison ministry, orphan ministry, as well as the public schools. Our days were full. Between our preparation time, travel time, and presentation times, we were working 10-12 hours a day, seven days a week. It was a joy to do God's work, but we were starting to feel a little stretched.

God knew what we needed and had been preparing the hearts of another couple who would follow His call to Russia. We didn't know them well. We had only met them once in Moscow. They were with a group on a short-term mission trip. I took the opportunity to tell that group we needed help, and that they should consider serving long-term in Kostroma. One couple on the bus accepted my challenge.

In September 1993, Curt and Debi Eyman joined us to help minister to the people of Kostroma. The Eymans were American Christians, not ministers by trade, but they had a heart for missions. They quit their jobs (Curt was working for UPS, and Debi worked as a bookkeeper) to come to work with us for a year. Curt and Debi added a lot to the team and helped lighten the load so that we could all minister more effectively. Curt and Debi are still a part of the

*Curt Eyman (white shirt, center) with a group
from the prison ministry*

ministry of Mission to Russia today, with Curt serving
on the Board of Directors.

Once we were settled in at the House of Nature,
we were able to accomplish so much more than we
could when we had a space of our own. We spent a
lot of our time preparing—preparing lessons, sermons, classes, but ultimately, in all these things, we
were preparing hearts to accept Jesus as Lord and
Savior. With a place of our own, we were able to host
more events, not just on Sundays, but also during the
week. We were excited that we were now able to host
our first Vacation Bible School. Emmanuel Christian
Church in Stoneboro, Pennsylvania partnered with
our church and brought a group of about 20 people.
They also brought all the lessons and supplies needed

to present the gospel to over 150 students. Everyone involved had a great time. Following VBS, many children started coming to Sunday school every week. After the group from Emmanuel Christian Church volunteered to lead VBS, our people were able to see what VBS looked like. This gave Ginny the opportunity to train teachers and helpers, equipping our church to hold a VBS on our own next time.

Preparing lessons for children in particular was rather challenging in Russia. There were no Christian materials available at that time, nothing written in their language. We had to take American storybooks and Bible pictures and make our own lessons from scratch. Any material, worksheet, or craft we gave each child had to be made by hand. Teaching in camps, orphanages, schools, and Sunday school, some weeks we taught over 1,000 people. In addition to making copies for every person, we had to have all the work translated into Russian. We wore out a copy machine about every two years. All this took place from our living room in our apartment until we moved into the House of Nature.

Traveling with all these materials was tricky. We traveled by city bus because we had no transportation of our own. Carrying so many supplies on a city bus was no easy feat. It wasn't long before God provided a better way for us to bring supplies with us. Three men from three different churches visited Russia and served with us for a month. They saw the need and God moved their hearts to leave us with enough money to buy a car for transporting these materials. It was a great blessing, and once again, we knew that God was providing for us in miraculous ways.

GINNY:

*Visiting a women's minimum security prison was a new experience for us. We brought in the flannel graph board to teach with, and within a few minutes, 200 inmates were waiting for us to begin! The silent, unwavering attention we received was remarkable. It was as if they stopped breathing to hear the good news of Jesus without hindrance.*

*After the service, we gave them toothbrushes and toothpaste, along with little bottles of lotion that had been sent with us from the States. A few ladies wanted to show me where they lived, so I followed them to the barrack-type dormitories. We had some great conversations over the next few months. Then one day we were told the Russian Orthodox Church was going to take over ministering to the women's prison. I was so disappointed. I received letters for a time, and some of the women I met in the prison came to our church upon being released.*

With our church starting to really come together, I felt led to prepare some of our members for church leadership through in-depth study of Scripture. I set up a 3-year program of college-like classes. We were going to study through the entire Bible. We met four nights a week, three hours a night, for three years. Thirteen people committed to the class, and no one missed a session unless they were ill. They were hungry for God's Word and had no desire to miss a class.

Out of these classes, God raised up the first three elders of our church, as well as other leaders for other ministry areas. The first three elders were Paul Hrabrav, Boris Lukmanov, and Vladimir Denishev. We partnered with the International Bible Seminary in Independence, Missouri, which granted degrees to those participating in the program. The program ran for about 10 years, with Vladimir and Boris leading classes after they completed the program themselves.

We were not afraid to try different ways to minister. We held a weekend seminar for family relations. We had plays, concerts, and children's Christmas programs. As Ginny began preparing for our first Christmas play in 1993, she found that most had never heard the story of Jesus' birth! So, she first had to teach them the story. Then, she put together costumes and taught them about the culture at the time Jesus was born.

It was such a blessing to teach people about the birth of Christ. We felt so humbled and blessed to get to tell them the beautiful story we knew so well and see their reaction to hearing it for the first time. We were reminded why God had called us at this time in this country, and we gave Him all the glory. The first Christmas play was a great success as many lives were blessed to see the wonderful story acted out by children.

## *The Lukmanovs*

Ginny and I were teaching the Bible at a Russian English camp when we met Sasha. Alexander Lukmanov, who goes by Sasha, was one of many young people who accepted the Lord and was baptized. Oftentimes, those who were baptized at the camps we visited would return home to their families who knew nothing about Jesus or what their child had done or what it meant.

There was little we could do to follow up with them, so we had to leave it in God's hands, knowing we may never see them again. Those running the camp would give us a list of their names, but no other contact information.

One Sunday out of the blue, Sasha (whom we recognized from the camp) attended our church service. Sasha also began attending Sunday school and

*Sasha Lukmanov and his family*

was captivated, more so than most young people were. He could also speak English better than most of the other children. He soon brought his mom, sister, and brother, and as a family they became regular attenders.

Then after weeks and weeks, one Sunday his father came. Sasha had brought his whole family to Jesus. Through weeks of teaching, questions, and answers, one by one his mom, sister, brother, and father were all baptized. They were the first complete family to follow Jesus and be baptized at Kostroma Christian Church.

None of us, not Boris or Inna, Sasha's father and mother, could have known what would happen as they became part of the church. Boris went on to be a pastor for many years, and Inna served as a children's ministry leader and a bookkeeper for the church.

Sasha grew so quickly and eagerly in his faith. He began learning the guitar and piano so that he could lead us in worship, becoming our first praise team leader at the age of 14. His father, Boris, had been an alcoholic, a heavy smoker, and an abuser to his family. When he came to the Lord, he immediately gave it all up to serve God and his family. He and Inna both attended the nightly Bible classes together. Inna volunteered with Ginny teaching Sunday school, and after a few years, she became the Sunday school leader. She went on to also train others to teach Sunday school. Three years after coming to the church, Boris became one of the first elders. He was known as the counseling elder, and people could come to for edification and encouragement.

Sasha continued to grow spiritually, studying English and the Bible throughout high school. He felt called to be a preacher, so we arranged for him to go to Bible College in America. He chose to attend St. Louis Christian College and graduated with a degree in preaching.

After obtaining his degree, he returned to Russia and moved to Gus Khrustalny to preach at a small Christian church there. Located about 200 miles from Kostroma, Gus (pronounced "goose") had a population of about 80,000 people. Max Goins, a missionary from Joplin, Missouri started a church with a small group of people in 1992, and then Sasha joined them after college in 2000. As of 2016, Sasha has been there about 16 years. After only eight years, Kostroma Christian Church already had a "Timothy" preaching in Russia.

## The Denisichevs

When Vladimir and Lena Denisichev first came to a church service, they sat in the back row, but they gradually moved forward until one week they were sitting on the front row. They attended church regularly, and soon also attended the evening Bible classes. They lived by faith in Jesus and learned and grew quickly in their faith. Three years after they first came to the church, Vladimir was chosen to be an elder, and was elected as the first Russian pastor of Kostroma Christian Church, sharing in preaching and other church business. Later on, Vladimir was a major contributor to starting a Christian school, overseeing the building of the school facilities. His wife, Lena, became the principal of the school and was one of the main teachers for Sunday school.

## *Sofia and Slava Plavinskaya*

We noticed Sofia one Sunday morning as she and her son, Slava, came in to the worship service. The fright was apparent on their faces. They left as soon as the service was over, so we weren't able to speak to them. The next Sunday they returned, and this time we met them. Sofia had a lot of reservations, but she wanted to learn what this church was all about. Slava was in his 20s, but he remained in his mother's care due to a childhood accident that impaired his mental ability.

We found out that Sofia and Slava were Muslim, but it was clear they had never known true joy or community. Her own family shunned her because of Slava. Sofia was lonely and bitter, yet they kept coming back. Each week, Sofia spent more time visiting with people and she began to make friends.

About two years after she started attending, Sofia accepted Christ, was baptized, and was made new. Her whole demeanor transformed. She changed to a positive, smiling, joyful person, and became an exceptional greeter in the church, with her son by her side. We feel so blessed to believe in a God who accepts us just as we are, even when our own families won't. God saw Sofia and Slava, and loved them and accepted them as His children.

*Alex Gribov and his family*

## *Alex Gribov*

Our interpreters, who studied at a university in Kostroma, were enthusiastic about inviting their peers to church. One of those students invited Alex Gribov, who was also studying English at university. A major selling point for him was the opportunity to practice speaking English with Americans. Alex went to the church for two years before accepting Christ. When asked about his testimony he said, "Looking back and thinking about what was the main thing which helped me to accept Christ, I understand that it was not the Bible or numerous sermons, but it was Ron and Ginny's faith and personal example." Alex would later become an elder and administrator, a valuable asset to the church and its people. He continues to be the administrator of the Christian school and an elder at the church to this day.

## Ministering to Neighboring Cities

We were witnessing God work in the lives of everyone coming to Kostroma Christian Church. Curt, Debi, Ginny, and I were not the only ones with a passion to serve. Our church body felt that call as well. We received invitations from different towns to come and present the gospel, and felt fully equipped to do just that.

We went to a town called Krasnoye-na-Volge to lead some evening meetings in the public school. In Sussanino we had several meetings for children and adults. A large group would leave from the church to go to these towns and show them Christ through song, teaching, fellowship, and prayer. Both of these towns were fairly close to Kostroma, less than a day's journey away.

Alexandria, a woman who visited our church once, invited us to the town in which she lived. It was a small city called Soligalich, about 200 miles north of Kostroma. She had heard about our church and came to see who and what we were. When the service was over, Alexandria told us she hoped someday to see an evangelistic church started in her town and asked if we could visit there to share the gospel.

Soligalich was home to about 8,000 people, and was way off the beaten path. Even by Russian standards the roads leading to her hometown were rough! It took seven hours to make the trip by bus. To paint a picture of the simplicity of this town, the only running water in the whole town was at one centrally located bathhouse. It was like going back to the 1930s or 1940s in America. Although we didn't realize it at the time, this trip was a special one.

GINNY:

*Alexandria's story was quite remarkable. Her parents had been Christians and had been sent to prison during the revolution. She was one of the few underground Christians who had continued to grow up in the Christian faith during the Communist reign and had always desired for a church to be established in her small town.*

*It was remarkable because we were the first Americans to be in this town, and I could feel everyone staring at us. We went by a building that was only partly finished. Alexandria said she had always dreamed of that building being finished and turned into a house of prayer. We asked her how old the building was. She said "Oh, it's the newest in town. I'd say about*

*200 years old." Oh! The whole country of America wasn't much older than that.*

*On Thursday, when we walked into the auditorium we were amazed. Four hundred people were waiting there. We began the service with a testimony. Then, I sang and told a story with the flannel graph. I then took the children to another room, while Ron preached to the adults. We did not fit in the room we went to. It was clear there was no way everyone would be able to spread out and color, so we tried to figure out another place to go to. These kids had never seen crayons before and were more than eager to color.*

*As we changed rooms, I have to assume that the children were afraid I would run out of pictures or crayons or something, because they all began to surge forward at once. They actually broke the door off the doorframe. It was a bit terrifying. Thankfully, nobody was hurt and we had enough material for everyone. The service ended with six ladies accepting the Lord. Ron baptized them at the bathhouse.*

*Upon arriving at the bus station to return home to Kostroma, we found three men lying under the front of the bus working with a blowtorch. This didn't give us a secure feeling. They said it would take an hour or so to repair so we might as well go into the station and wait. I saw Alexandria holding a small book in her hands. She was softly singing, and I actually recognized the melody of the song. I began to sing along with her. She told me the book she had was an old Russian hymnal she had kept for years. She gave the hymnal to me, and I treasure it as a remembrance of a wonderful time in Soligalich.*

*Finally, the bus was fixed or at least fixed to a useable state. I guess they were having trouble with the gears, so when we slowed down to a near stop it would just jerk along instead of actually stop. They would slow down because people were always asking to get off the bus along the way in the middle of the countryside. Most lived nearby somewhere and the buses were their only mode of transportation. Sometimes it would "stop" for people standing on the side of the road waiting for a ride. People were running along the side of the bus, some with children in their arms, and leaping on when the doorway was clear. That's how it was for the entire 7-hour trip.*

*Ron and I returned to Soligalich the next February just to spend a day with those ladies who had been baptized. We had a wonderful reunion and spent the day studying God's Word and praying together. One of the ladies asked us what she should do. Her husband was a Muslim and was not happy with her decision to become a Christian. I took her to the Scripture in 1 Peter where Peter encourages women to live their lives before their husbands in such a way that their husbands who did not believe would be won by the example lived before them. I didn't know what else to say other than to promise to continue to remember her in prayer as she lived to glorify God with her life.*

*Those ladies made the 7-hour bus trip a couple of times during the next year just to attend services and have fellowship with our church women. Unfortunately, time and events sepa-*

*rated us from returning to their town. We held on to the fact that the gospel had been preached, seeds had been planted, and there was a small harvest.*

*Now, I must fast forward seven years. We were standing in front of the church in Kostroma visiting with a friend when a car passing by came to the screeching halt. We looked up and saw a lady jump out of the car and gave Ron the biggest hug. As soon as she began to speak we recognized her as the lady from Soligalich for whose husband we had been praying. "Come, come," she said, "I want you to meet my husband." She introduced him not only as her husband, but also as the pastor of their church in Soligalich, which was now running about 50 people. Praise the Lord! What a story of transformation!*

Ginny and I never anticipated what God would accomplish through only two visits to that tiny town. It seems ridiculous how we underestimated what God could do, but we were blessed to have been a part of such a great story that points to the glory of God. It is through experiences like this that we were continually sustained and affirmed in our work for the Lord.

## *Moving Again*

In 1995, after two years at the House of Nature, our rental agreement was coming to an end. We had to decide whether to stay and commit to a higher rental rate, or find another place, possibly a place of our very own. Since we were outgrowing the House of Nature, we began to look around for property. Also, the people of the church expressed interest in having a building of our own. With our own building, we would have access to rooms 24 hours a day, and the congregation believed the community would be more open to the idea of coming to the church. It felt right to us to build our own facility. We found a property in a good location, and we got an architect to draw up some plans. We felt this was right, but we didn't have much money to put toward it. Money would be essential to fund a construction plan.

By this point, the church was about three years old and had grown to over 150 people. However, half of them were without work, about a fourth of them were on a small pension, and the rest were making the equivalent of $50 or less per month. When the offering plate was passed each week, people gave generously. Unfortunately, when it was all counted it would not amount to more than $20 or so.

GINNY:

*Many in our congregation were living off of pensions, which amounted to about $38 a month, and they were concerned about tithing. Some months they didn't actually receive their pensions. So, they asked if they could bring produce from their gardens as a tithe. We talked about how God loves a cheerful giver (2 Corinthians 9:7), and I told them God would accept their gifts as long as they were given with sincere hearts in worship.*

*Our offering table began to take on a new look, with rubles along with potatoes, cabbage, carrots, and apples. After each service, we would offer the produce to anyone who had need. It was a beautiful display of God's people giving back to God and taking care of one another.*

There was no way we could come up with enough money for a building on our own. I planned a trip to America to visit our supporting churches and share with them our desire to have our own church building. We were going to need about $100,000 over a two-year period. In faith, we believed this hope would become a reality once we shared our vision with our supporters.

I embarked on a five week visit to the States. I visited all of our supporting churches reporting the progress we were seeing in Russia and expressing the dream we had to get our own building. I returned to Kostroma with $20,000 raised upfront along with pledges for the remaining $80,000 over the next two years. Back in Russia, together as a congregation we rejoiced in the blessings that God provided for us.

To our dismay, it was not long before we learned the property we had chosen was, according to the Orthodox church, too close to an Orthodox church. The Orthodox church used everything in their power to stop our purchase of that property. We would not be allowed to build a church there. It was such disappointing news, especially because God had already provided the money we needed.

## *Relentless Renovating*

So, we had the money, but no place to spend it. We prayed daily for God to lead us to a permanent place. Faithful as he always is, in no time at all God led us to a large two-story building at the edge of town. This building was about 80 years old. It was originally built to be an Orthodox church, but during the revolution the Communists destroyed it. It was later remodeled and used as a place to build ships. Still later, it served as a combination theater and library.

*The building before it was renovated,*
*home to Kostroma Christian Church*

When we found it, it had been abandoned for several years. It was a wreck. All the windows and water lines were missing. All the electrical wires and wooden flooring had been stolen. The boilers for heating the building were completely rusted and useless. The building looked dilapidated, covered with burn marks and with plaster falling off. Weeds had taken over the yard. It was not what we had in mind, definitely not our first choice, but it seemed God could use this old building that no one else wanted anymore.

We prayed and prayed and prayed about this decision. We had many meetings to discuss whether this was the right way to go. In these meetings we all felt that though this would be an incredibly grueling process, God was leading us to follow His plan for this building, for His thoughts are not our thoughts and His ways are not our ways (Isaiah 55:8).

We were very careful going into this project. We talked as a congregation about how much work we would be doing and that we would all have to work as a team to bring this building up to code. The church agreed, and we purchased the building for only $20,000. This was a bargain. This building was three times the size of the first building we were planning to build. Twenty thousand dollars was the exact amount we had raised in America.

In order to re-construct this building, we would need about $100,000 total, the same amount pledged to us for the original plan. We contacted all those who had given or promised money for the building project and let them know the change in our plans. With no objections, we began the renovation. It was really only possible with the money we had raised because the ruble had lost its value to the dollar.

We started the remodel by scraping the inside walls down because they had been frozen over several winters. We put in new floors and windows in all the rooms. The whole building had to be rewired and light fixtures installed. We ran all new plumbing. We put heating units in every room, as well as a new boiler system for gas rather than coal. Because the building had no modern facilities in it, we built bathrooms completely from scratch. The outside of the building had to be re-stuccoed, and the whole inside had to be painted. The roof had to be replaced. It was a major overhaul. But it was one we were happy to take up. The Lord had provided a spacious, affordable building for His people.

One element was challenging: the church needed a baptistery. It was not as if we could just go out and buy one. It would require some creative thinking. We tried to put one in made out of tile, but it simply didn't work. The people we were working with had never even seen a permanently placed baptistery before, let alone know how to build one from scratch. We decided to take the portable fiberglass baptistery we had been using for the past few years and try to give it a permanent place. We made a steel frame and set it inside. Then, we rigged it for water and drainage. It was a little unorthodox, but it worked great! To this day, the original baptistery is being used in the church building.

It took several months to get the building to the point where we could use it for church functions. We were desperate to get it ready, especially because we had to pay rent at the House of Nature while still spending money for the renovation of the building.

We knew the building project would take a year or more, considering most of the work was done by volunteers. The thought of paying rent and paying to renovate was daunting to say the least, but God continued to provide funds. By the time we were able to use the building, all bills were paid! We had no debt and no lingering payments!

GINNY:

*I was doing laundry in the bathtub, a few things every day or two. My body was not used to this kind of work and I was feeling it. In fact, my back was hurting badly, which I think was the result of trying to ring out towels by hand. Our friend Sergey noticed I was in a lot of pain and told me that he would bring me a cure.*

*The next morning he came and handed me a large sack. I looked inside. It looked like dog hair. Sure enough, that's what it was! He had gone home, bathed his dog, and shaved its stomach. I was supposed to wrap the hair in a towel and tie it around my middle so it was up against my back. In theory, I guess that makes sense as it would hold in my body heat, but I wasn't too sure about wearing the dog hair. But because he had gone to so much trouble to help me, I did as he said. No one will ever know if it was the dog hair or the aspirin that gave me relief.*

## *Home, Freezing Home*

Though it wasn't finished by a long shot, in early autumn of 1995 we enthusiastically moved our services into our new building. The walls were not yet painted. The floors weren't finished yet. The heating system was due to be up and running soon. The furnace would be ready in no time. So, thinking everything would be ready shortly, we moved in.

We had made wooden benches for the main room where we would gather as a congregation. We had found a good deal on used school desks and chairs for the Sunday school classrooms, and with our baptistery in place, we had all we needed. We rejoiced that God had provided us with a great facility and prayed that the heat would come on by the time it was wintery cold, which in Kostroma can be as early as October.

We saw a great turnout in worship and many newcomers every week. It was during these first few months in the new building that we ordained the first elders of the church and selected Vladimir as the first Russian preacher. October came and the heating system was not yet functioning. During the ordination of elders, everyone was wearing hats and coats. October led to November and November to December. By now it was seriously cold—below freezing.

*The church building after renovation (1996)*

We could see the frost on the inside walls of the auditorium as we worshipped while wearing boots, coats, hats and gloves. It was quite a sight as the auditorium was filled every Sunday with folks dressed like this. Eventually, we asked the congregation if we should dismiss early on Sundays, but they didn't want to, they wanted to go the full 3-4 hours. So we did— cold, numbing fingers and toes and all!

Finally, in the middle of January the heat came on! It was a wonderful day! The heat came on at the beginning of the week, giving the building time to thaw out from the past few months. We went into the auditorium to check how things were going with the heat working, and we saw an amazing sight. Mist was coming from the walls and ceiling due to the drastic change in temperature. Through the mist, there were butterflies flying all around. It was a stunning display, going from a cold cocoon-like existence into a totally new warm experience, like one who comes out of sin and darkness into His marvelous light.

Moving into a building of our own marked another new era for Kostroma Christian Church. As we had hoped, the church had become a Russian church with Russian people working together to lead other Russians to Christ. We were still there, but it was now so much bigger than our own efforts. They had their own building, leadership, teachers, and worship team. Together we were ministering to about 300 adults and children each Sunday.

GINNY:

*It was a blessing to attend a women's retreat in Moscow, as well as teach a class there. Along with a few women from our church, I traveled to Moscow for the weekend-long conference. When the time came for me to speak Friday night, I was exhausted from the past week and all the traveling. So, I spoke for about an hour, and then later went to bed, feeling upset. I had not done the best I could.*

*The next day, a woman came to talk to me. She was invited by a friend to the retreat, and this was the first time she was around a group of Christians. She was amazed and intrigued. She said that my words from the previous night spoke to her heart. My eyes started to well up.*

*Later, I heard that she spent the next evening asking her friend about God, studying the Bible, and on Sunday morning, she was baptized into Christ. She lived way up north by the Baltic Sea, and didn't know of any Christians there, so several women loaded her up with a new Bible, Bible study books, and pamphlets to take home with her.*

# Chapter 3

## *Back to America*

AFTER FOUR YEARS, THE CHURCH was doing really well. People were walking by faith, serving the Lord, and sharing Christ with others. In light of what our church body was doing, Ginny and I began to feel as though we might not be needed any longer. It was always our goal to bring the church to a place of self-sufficiency, run by Russians, and truly be a Russian church. I had been sharing the responsibility of preaching on Sundays with two others, Boris and Vladimir.

The three of us held a meeting to discuss this question: was I needed any longer? We all agreed that if they could continue preaching, with me stepping down, there would be no need for an interpreter. The interpreting was the last evidence that this was an "American mission" aspect happening. Without the interpreting, people visiting might not realize that this was a church planted through American mission. It became clear that if I wasn't needed to preach, I wasn't needed to be at the church at all. It was time to allow the new church to be on its own.

I was apprehensive about leaving, hoping these new Christians were mature enough to handle running the church, to deal with the persecution that would continue due to the Orthodox church. I was anxious, but I had faith in them and that God would protect them.

After four-and-a-half years of building relationships and making Kostroma home, it was with many tears and emotional goodbyes that we packed our personal belongings and flew back to the United States. For a time, we stayed in our son's basement in Wichita, Kansas until we could find a permanent place to live. It was a good time for us, because we had not seen our grandsons since they had been born.

Leroy and Gwen Herder were a godsend, especially during our time stateside. They had taken a trip to Kostroma and led a wonderful marriage workshop attended by almost everyone in the congregation. When we came back to the U.S., we were without a car and the Herders gave us one. Later on, there would come a time when they would give us a second car. They were a special blessing, not just to us personally, but to the whole ministry.

I looked for employment as a preacher, and heard about a church hiring in Pennsylvania. Ginny and I drove 1,500 miles so that I could interview there, and I was hired on the spot. I would be the preaching minister at First Christian Church of Meadville. As if that wasn't blessing enough, we now had a place to live because the church had a parsonage. What's more, our new church was pleased to support Kostroma Christian Church both in prayer and financially. They even sent Ginny and me there for two weeks one summer to help with a Vacation Bible School.

We had a great reunion, back with our friends in Kostroma. It was also a good opportunity to discuss face-to-face the possibility of building a Christian school. This project would require a lot of money and paperwork. This had been a vision of the church leadership and mine before we had left Kostroma, and now they wanted to make those dreams a reality. Up to this point, several churches in Russia had tried to start a Christian school, but no one was able to get paperwork signed and approved.

It was estimated to cost at least $100,000 to build

a Christian school, along with all the paperwork signed by all state, city, and educational governments needed. The church decided to at least try, and if it was meant to be, it would happen. If Vladimir, the current pastor, could get all the paperwork signed by all parties, we would take the proposition to the supporting churches to see if we could raise the money. I was fairly confident it wouldn't happen, that the paperwork would not go through. To my own surprise within a few months, the forms to operate a Christian school went through. Everything was approved. So, we shared our plans with our supporting churches. Again, we would need about $100,000.

The response was overwhelming. Thousands of dollars were being sent in, along with promises of thousands more to come. It was decided we would not go into debt to build, but the school would be built as funds came in. We trusted that God would provide the funds in His time. This required some patience, but it was a smart financial decision for sure. Because of the amount of funds coming in from individuals to fund the new building, it was at that time when Mission to Russia became a 501(c)(3) organization—a tax-exempt, non-profit organization recognized by the government.

One day, I received what was basically a cry for help from the church leadership in Kostroma.

Because there was so much going on with the church, school, and the Bible college, they needed help. They were overwhelmed by the workload and hoped that I would come back and be the administrator of the Bible College, and that Ginny would teach Bible classes once the Christian school was built. This door seemed to be wide open. We hadn't ignored any opportunities thus far and we weren't about to start now. I found myself going to a group of church leaders for the second time and announcing that we were being led back into the mission field. They were very understanding and were behind us in our decision. We had been living in America for about three years.

## Back to Russia

In 1999, we were headed back to Kostroma with little money and no place to live. But this time was nowhere near as difficult. This time we had a church family to join and work with. Our housing situation was taken care of before we ever left the States. An elder from the church in Meadville invited Ginny and me to dinner one evening. At that meal, he presented us with an envelope that contained enough money to not only buy an apartment, but also to furnish it. It was an emotional evening for us.

We will be eternally grateful to him and his wife for what they did. They would not want to be named in this writing, so though they remain unnamed, it is important that we share how God was continually faithful in providing for us through His people. It was such a blessing to go back to Russia knowing we had enough money to get an apartment.

## *Light to the World Christian Academy*

While the school building was being constructed, classes met in a couple of rooms at the church. The first year began with one first grade class. The second year, those students went to second grade, and a new class of first graders came in. Then, we would add one grade each year until we offered classes for all grade levels.

The building construction began in the winter of 1999. Although we trusted God that the school would be built as money was available, it was still remarkable that not once did we run out of funds to purchase materials or pay the workers. As I mentioned before, it was estimated that building the academy would cost about $100,000. However, inflation was still on the rise, and there were some costs we didn't foresee. The final cost for the project was about $500,000, five

*Construction of Light to the World Christian Academy*

times what we had anticipated. Nevertheless, God provided every cent. During those two years of construction, we were blessed with half a million dollars from our supporters. We had no need to borrow a single ruble or dollar.

Looking at the finished product—the three stories of classrooms and an official size gymnasium—we could only praise the Lord for providing us with so much. We named it Light to the World Christian Academy with the hope that our school would raise up children to be a light in this dark country.

We were in the process of moving back to Russia just as the construction was starting. We quickly found a flat near the church. The minute we got settled, we were up and going. Things were happening so fast. There was so much to do. The senior pastor

*Light to the World building on the left,*
*Kostroma Christian Church on the right*

Vladimir was in charge of overseeing the building process, so the majority of his time and energy were spent on that project. This meant many of his other responsibilities were left undone. It was my pleasure to come alongside him and help with those things.

I took up leading the Bible College, now meeting five nights a week, three hours a night. I shared the job of teaching with two elders. Working hand in hand with the church leadership in the ministry of the church, we met weekly to ensure issues and most importantly, that people were in good care. Ginny took on teaching Bible classes for Light to the World, about eight classes each week.

In addition, she was working with the ladies' group that she had started during our first four years there, teaching them once a week. The group grew to about 30 women during this time. In what little spare

*LTTW students attending a Vacation Bible School (2001)*

time she had, Ginny also developed training classes for the teachers at the academy.

After two years of construction with classes held in the church building, the school building was completed. In September 2001, classes began in the new school building, with first through third grades offered at that time. Unfortunately, the church simply did not have enough money to fund an entire school on its own, so a student sponsorship program was organized with people and churches in the States. Each person or church contributed monthly the amount needed for a student to attend the academy. They also had the opportunity to correspond through letters and visit their sponsor student in Kostroma through trips organized by Mission to Russia.

In the early days of LTTW Christian Academy, a

*Light to the World students (2014)*

couple from Texas moved to Kostroma to serve with the church and school. Jeff and Suzie Wollman were teachers, both specializing in computer graphics, and they had experience teaching Christian ethics. They took on the task of teaching computer classes at the academy as well as offering evening courses on graphics and web design for adults. In the past, they had primarily worked in Russian orphanages, and they continued to work with orphans while they were in Kostroma. Even though they were not able to be in Russia more than a year and a half, they made a huge impact in their time there.

The school is one of few Christian private schools in all of Russia accredited by the Russian educational system. This is significant because it means that the graduates of LTTW Christian Academy can go to any Russian university following graduation. Light to the World has become a rather prestigious school. They are known in their region for offering a solid education, specifically in English studies. The school has ranked first place of all schools in their region twice, in 2012 and 2014. This ranking is determined through testing taken by students each spring in every school in their region (about the size that qualifies as a state in America).

There is even a waiting list to get into LTTW. Because of the size of the classrooms, each grade is limited to 15 students. Each class remains full every year. When a student moves or transfers, another comes in their place. Incoming students must pass certain tests to gain admittance into the school. Because the academy offers difficult, high level classes, it is not suitable for everyone. The school hosts about 125 students in total.

## Student Ministry

In the first couple of years after we moved back to Russia, many new ministries began to thrive. Perhaps the most significant development was the beginning of the youth group. We recognized that for the church to continue to exist in the future, we had to prioritize pouring into young people.

We only had a handful of students attending the church regularly, so we decided to bring them together in a small group setting in our apartment once a week. For a while it was a small group, no more than 12 students. None of them attended the same school (Russian public schools are based in neighborhoods), and we wanted to offer an opportunity for them to get to know each other better and build mutually edifying relationships. They came at 6:30 p.m. on Saturday nights. We always had an interactive game of some sort just to have some fun, followed by devotions led by Ginny. Then the guitars would come out, and the singing would begin. Oh, how they loved to sing!

One of Ginny's favorite things was preparing a snack each week. She introduced them to all sorts of yummy snacks: popcorn, soda, pizza, chip dip, and chocolate chip cookies. We also decorated sugar cookies at Christmas and dyed eggs at Easter. It's true: the way to a teenager's heart is through their stomach! They loved all the new foods we showed them.

It wasn't long before they invited others to join us, and we began to outgrow our space. Even though our flat was a decent size by Russian standards, it was not very big. Soon, we had teenagers everywhere, on the furniture and even sitting on the floor. It is a cultural tradition to remove your shoes when entering someone's home in Russia, and our entryway began to look comical as the pairs of shoes piled higher.

We were getting to the point of hosting about 30 kids and completely maxed out our space. The teens themselves came up with a solution they would like. They asked us if perhaps we could instead meet at the church building so they could invite more people, and they wanted me to preach full sermons. We were thrilled to help them as they wanted to share the gospel with their friends.

As requested, we started meeting in the church auditorium on Saturday nights, with at least half an hour of singing worship. Then, I would preach, and communion was served. Ginny prepared dinner for the group once a month. Within a few months of moving the group to the church, we saw an average attendance of about 60 kids. Ginny and I were not the ones out there inviting people. It was the teens. We were so proud of them.

After the service was over, most kids would stick around to play volleyball, or gather around the piano to continue singing. As we looked around the auditorium, we would see pockets of people with heads together, Bibles opened, praying. It was no surprise to us that we grew.

On top of that, the students understood that being at the youth service didn't mean skipping church Sunday morning. In fact, many of them served in some way by either helping the Sunday school teachers, the worship team, or serving as greeters. Some simply met for an hour before church to start praying for the service. For the most part, we didn't have to spend much effort in teaching them these things. They were ambitious and eager to serve God.

Another area that the youth took upon themselves was mentoring. Ginny was teaching Bible classes on Wednesday evenings to women at the church. She started noticing a few young ladies from ages 16-18 were always there and taking notes. After class, some younger teenage girls would come into the church building. So, she inquired about what the girls were doing, and the older girls explained that they were holding their own class, passing on what they were learning to the younger girls using notes from Ginny's class. When she asked them about this, they simply said, "The Bible tells us that the older women should teach the younger. You teach us, and now we share those teachings the younger girls."

One of our fondest memories began when Ginny had a group of girls over to our flat for tea. There were 16 girls there between the ages of 15-18. They were discussing God's plan for marriage. They were serious about it. One of them expressed concern because there weren't very many Christian men their age, and they wanted to marry Christian men. Gwen Herder was visiting Kostroma and mentoring along with Ginny. The girls told Ginny and Gwen that they had an idea and wanted to see what they thought of it. They had decided to dedicate every Wednesday as a day to pray specifically for God to bring young men to the church so they could become Christians to be God-honoring husbands for them someday. Ginny and Gwen not only thought it was a wonderful plan, but also agreed to join them in prayer.

A few short months after that meeting, God answered those prayers and brought some young men to the church who would become great husbands and what's more, leaders in the church.

## Ilya and Sasha

One Sunday morning during the invitation time, a young man came forward and gave himself to the Lord. We didn't know him and were pretty sure we had never seen him before. We learned he was one of the most notorious drug users in the city. His reputation spread through the congregation, and parents were warning their children to stay away from him.

*Left to right: Sasha Zhurin, Michael Green & Ilya Sheptunev*

For several years, a woman had been attending services at the church and had asked for prayer for her son who was caught up in a life of drugs. The young man, now 17, was named Ilya Sheptunev.

After he gave his life to the Lord, Ilya also started coming to our Saturday night youth service. For a while he came alone. Then, one week he brought his friend, Sasha Zhurin, who had been known as his partner in crime. His friend Sasha soon accepted Christ as well. Their transformation was incredible by the grace of God. Both of these young men learned and grew very quickly. They even led worship for youth services.

An excellent guitarist and singer, Ilya later became the church worship leader. Ilya and Sasha attended the Bible college in the church, soaking up the Scriptures. They both graduated from the Bible college, and became leaders, not just of the youth, but the church. You can read their full testimonies in the back of this book.

## 1 Peter 3:15 Club

During the height of the student ministry growth, some of the teens came to us requesting to learn more about evangelism and how they could share Christ with their friends. We set up a club and called it the 1 Peter 3:15 Club. This verse states, "But in your hearts revere Christ as Lord. Always be prepared to give an answer to everyone who asks you to give the reason for the hope that you have. But do this with gentleness and respect." We began meeting Sunday afternoons to discuss evangelism, using key verses in the Bible. We made it a priority to memorize these key verses that could lead people to accepting Christ. We taught them how to integrate Scripture along with their personal testimonies.

After several weeks of study and memorization, we began to see real results. Everyone participating in the club was encouraged to share Christ with someone each week. Then, at our club meetings we would talk about how it went. About 30 students were going out and witnessing to their friends every week. This was a large contributor to the growth of the youth group. These teenagers didn't just go to church, they were being the church. They took it upon themselves to follow Christ's call to live a life of faith.

## *Generous Donations*

During this same time, student ministry wasn't the only success story we experienced. God was blessing Kostroma Christian Church in many ways. We received some substantial donations at a time when people were in great need. Dr. Carl and Dr. Cathy Meyer saw an opportunity to gather medical supplies through a national resource and ship them to Kostroma. This was huge for our community. The healthcare system was lacking, to say the least. Although doctors in Russia were competent, they had little supplies with which to work.

The medical supplies gathered were not just small things. We did receive small supplies for treating cuts and burns, but we were also given baby incubators, X-ray machines, and other major machines. None of the equipment we received was new, but they had been completely refurbished to their original working condition and adapted to the electrical system in Russia. We calculated that the supplies donated were worth over a million dollars! When all the equipment finally reached Kostroma, we invited every doctor in Kostroma to come and collect what they needed. They were touched by the generosity. Some were stunned and speechless.

Times were tough for the Russian people. Food was expensive and in short supply. Many people were out of work, and we saw true hunger for the first time in our lives. Most people lived off gardens located somewhere out in the country. They had to depend on the rain for watering the plants and hope that disease would not ruin what they had planted.

At the National Missionary Convention (now called ICOM) in 2000, I visited the I.D.E.S. booth. The International Disaster Emergency Service is a parachurch organization of the Independent Christian churches that meets emergency needs around the world. I told them of the troubling conditions in Russia and the need for funds to buy food in Kostroma. I was asked to fill out an application for aid on the spot. In only a few weeks, their board had agreed to send $900 a month to MTR to buy food. With I.D.E.S.'s help, we were able to get food at a wholesale warehouse in large containers. We would bring that food to the church building and our people would package it in family size packs and hand them out to people from our church and in the community.

It's been said, "It takes a village to raise a child." Similarly, God continually reminded us that it takes more than two missionaries to make a church. God moved in the hearts of so many people, churches, and organizations to join with this mission work. We know for sure there were people and churches from Pennsylvania, Ohio, Illinois, Missouri, Texas, Minnesota, Nebraska, Kansas, Wyoming, Oklahoma, New Mexico, Colorado, California, and Oregon that came as short-term missionaries to serve in Kostroma.

We were supported by Bible colleges like St. Louis Christian College, Ozark Christian College, and the Christian Campus House ministry at Missouri State University. One year, the JCPenney company gave over 100 pairs of jeans to be distributed through our ministry. It didn't just take a village. God used people all over a nation to build this church. I could never be prideful about what was accomplished in Kostroma because so much was done without my hand being a part of it. I remained humble and worshipful.

## Church Community

We had so many opportunities to gather as brothers and sisters in Christ to simply enjoy life together. We had picnics where we would eat and then sit around and sing. We would sled and ski during the winter months. Ginny and I had a blast teaching our friends different American traditions that they had not experienced before, like roasting hot dogs and marshmallows over a fire, and how to play softball and basketball.

Teaching softball was more difficult than we thought, and comical, too. It was nearly impossible to teach people who had never before seen the game played. We explained the rules as plainly as we could and began a game. It may have been the longest pick-up game in softball history. This group of adults and teens were trying to play and understand the rules. Still, every play had to be stopped and rules re-explained. Finally, a man was up to bat and was the first to hit the ball. He started running. Boy, did he run. He ran to first base and kept on running straight ahead to a grove of trees that were a couple hundred feet away. Everyone nearly died of laughter.

## *Expanding the Leadership Team*

Vladimir and Boris, the church pastors, worked very hard to lead the church, but as the church grew, they needed additional help. With the congregation's blessings, Ilya Sheptunev, Sasha Zhurin, and Alex Gribov were added to the leadership team. These new leaders were very young in years, in their early twenties, and also young in Christian years. The plan was for Vladimir, Boris, and I to mentor and teach these young men and share responsibilities with them. Ilya and Sasha had experience preaching, so they joined in the preaching rotation on Sundays. The church was already used to multiple preachers, since Vladimir, Boris, and I all preached over the years.

In winter 2001, we heard some great news. Ilya and Sasha were engaged to two young ladies in the church. They were from the group of girls that met in our living room and prayed for young men to become Christians so they could marry Christian men. They set their double wedding plans for August 2002.

# Chapter 4

## *Troubling News*

IN 2002, GINNY AND I needed to travel to America to renew our visas and visit our supporting churches. We left in May with plans to return the last week of July to be back in time to perform the double wedding ceremony for Ilya, Sasha, and their fiancés. We had decided at this point, God willing, we would live in Russia for the rest of our lives. We would be in Kostroma not necessarily as missionaries, as that work was finished, but we would volunteer in the church to support the leaders.

We had a good time in America, visiting our son, his wife, and our two grandsons. We then traveled to churches, giving reports on the progress in Kostroma. We even attended the graduation ceremony of Sasha

Lukmanov at St. Louis Christian College. He left the week after his graduation, traveling back to Russia to serve at Gus Krustalny Christian Church.

Just before we were to return to Russia, we were at the North American Christian Convention. We were waiting for our visas to be renewed and looking forward to getting back to our church family in Russia. We had our bags packed for the trip and our return tickets purchased when we got a devastating phone call. We received the message that our visas were denied. We thought there was a mistake. We had never had any problems getting visa approval in the past. We tried calling the Russian embassy in charge of visa approval. They would not tell us why they denied us. They stated that they didn't have to tell us why we had been denied. We wrote official letters explaining our situation to the head of visa approval in Russia but never heard back. We were stuck in America possessing only two suitcases of clothing. Everything else was back in Russia.

This was not what we had planned. We didn't know what to do. And we felt bad for Ilya and Sasha and their future wives who had been waiting for our return to officiate their wedding. They actually put the weddings off for a few weeks, waiting to see if our visas were approved. Finally, when we saw no change, they were married by one of the church pastors.

For a time we lived in the St. Louis area near Curt and Debi Eyman. We attended Mid Rivers Christian Church, which had supported MTR, faithfully praying for us and the situation in Russia for many years. We rented an apartment, and I worked with the mission stateside traveling to churches and raising funds. Ginny went to work for JCPenney, having worked for them before we moved to Russia. Every six months we would re-apply for our visas, waiting for them to be approved. Months went by, then years, but no visas.

We moved for a short time to western Missouri where I filled in preaching for a church, then we finally settled down in Wichita, Kansas where our son lived. We purchased a double wide mobile home. By now, three years had passed and our hopes of returning to our ministry in Russia were growing dim as our visas were denied time after time. Since we had no savings, and all of our possessions had been left in Kostroma, we sold our flat. Some of our belongings were sent back to us piece by piece with short-term mission trips who visited Kostroma.

Short-term missionaries could get visas to visit Russia, but we found out that other full-time missionaries had also been denied Russian visas for the last few years. We weren't the only ones, which was a tiny bit comforting. We continued in corresponding with the church through email and Skype. We served on the Mission to Russia Board of Directors and did as much work as possible from America.

## *Difficult times*

As other issues arose, it was clear Satan was at work against the church in Kostroma, and not getting our visas was just part of it. Boris' wife Inna noticed discrepancies in the financial reports. Inna was the bookkeeper for the church. She asked Vladimir about it, who refused to give her a straight answer and shortly after, fired her and kept her from volunteering in other areas at the church. Following these events, Boris quickly resigned. He and Inna moved to Gus Khrustalny to help their son Sasha minister there.

In September 2004, the Mission to Russia Board of Directors removed Vladimir from his place of leadership. This caused some big losses for the church. Vladimir's wife Lena was the superintendent for Light to the World Christian Academy. The church lost two preachers and a superintendent all at once. Furthermore, Inna and Lena were leading the children's ministry, so with both of them stepping away, it was left to some volunteers to carry on without them.

Within a two-year period, the church came close to splitting. We felt helpless halfway across the world, with no way to get to them. It could have been the end of the work that so many people had supported and prayed for. The church was hurting. Their spirits were way down. But we praise God, for His work was not yet finished. The church struggled through for a few years, but slowly and surely healing took place.

The Mission to Russia Board of Directors made many steps to help the church continue to thrive. Alex Gribov was teaching English at the academy and became the new superintendent. Under his leadership the school has been and is doing very well. He managed the transition honorably, and leads the school well to this day.

Also, MTR board members made several short-term trips to Russia to help Ilya, Sasha, and Alex as well as the congregation to get back to the heart of what it means to be a church family, to allow God to work in their lives. John Canon, Tim Clark, Curt Eyman, and Ken Peterson in particular were a great help to the church's healing process.

*Helen leading worship at KCC, playing the keyboard*

## *Elena Morozova*

Elena Morozova (Helen to all the Americans who knows her) moved to Kostroma and started attending the church in June 1998. She was a mature Christian and stepped right in, volunteering in secretarial work and interpreting. She also taught English from day one of the academy. When Alex became superintendent, she stepped up to handle more English classes. She led worship and trained others in that area. She was, and is, an excellent interpreter and became the main voice between the Mission to Russia Board of Directors and the church in communicating with each other.

She is also the main interpreter between the

American sponsors and the students at the academy. She translates letters written between the sponsors and the students. Because of her knowledge of Scripture, she is an exceptional sermon interpreter. She is also the church's Sunday school director. She was a much needed influencer when the church was going through those difficult years, guiding others to make wise decisions and to rely on God. Helen continues to be a light to her students and her community in all she does.

## New Visa Laws

In 2008, after many attempts to secure a Russian visa over the span of six years, it finally happened! We were issued Russian visas, and we were allowed to go back to Russia again. It was slightly different this time, because the visa laws had changed. We could no longer spend a full year in Russia between visa renewals. The law stated that a foreign missionary could spend just 90 days at a time in Russia, and there had to be 90 days between each visit. So, we could visit for 90 days at a time, but there was no way we could return to live in Kostroma. It would be neither financially possible nor responsible. We had hoped that our visa approval would mean we could move back to serve our church as it was still in a state of healing. Unfortunately, it just was not going to happen. Although through the years, God had opened so many doors for us in Russia, it appeared that this door was closing.

With visa clearance secured, I decided to return for 90 days at a time for a year or two. While there, I would teach, train, counsel, and help the church leadership and its congregants any way I could. I stayed in a room in the church building and was available 24/7. I taught classes, preached, met with the leadership weekly, and had many counseling sessions with people in the church.

After three of these 90-day ministry sessions, Ginny joined me and we went back for 60 days during which she was able to reconnect with the ladies group, and encourage the Sunday school teachers. We were so proud of the young church leaders. They had grown spiritually despite, or possibly due to, the problems they had faced. They had gained much experience and maturity. They were great examples to the church body and their community. Through the fires of conflict, God had refined them to be the type of leaders Kostroma Christian Church needed.

During our 60-day visit, we informed the church we would no longer be able to partner with them in ministry in a semi-permanent way. We were of the age when our bodies were making it difficult to travel back and forth to Russia. On top of that, we knew they didn't really need us, as God had provided them with good leadership. We would hope to visit some in the future, but it was clear we weren't needed and physically couldn't keep up anymore. The church threw a huge going away celebration for us, and many tears were shed as people hung onto us. We held tightly to each other. It was not an easy goodbye.

This was the first time we left them with no plan of returning soon. Nineteen years earlier, we had begun the journey with no knowledge of the language or culture, no place to live. Today there is a flourishing church body made up of people of all generations, backgrounds, interests. They love the Lord and live to honor Him with their lives.

GINNY:

*We learned so much during our time in Russia. I think the most wonderful lesson was learning each and every day how faithful God is to His Word, His church, and His children. As Christians we all say we know that to be true. But I now KNOW and BELIEVE it is so, because He met our needs in every facet of life and ministry.*

*This showed true most evidently in the matter of prayer. I understand now why the Scriptures tell us to pray without ceas-*

*ing, because that is what I did in Kostroma. Every time I left our flat, and I walked the streets of the city, my mind was in constant communion with the Father for safety, protection, our ministry, and our friends. He guided me as I taught His Word to thousands of children and women. He provided me with the physical and emotional strength to live there.*

*Before I left for Kostroma in the beginning, I had confided in five ladies and asked if they would commit to pray daily, specifically for our health. I trusted the doctors who were well-educated to care for people, but they didn't have the necessary supplies and equipment. I knew I didn't want to spend any time in one of those hospitals. Knowing those ladies were praying, and God would honor their prayers, kept me from worrying about health. We were healthy all the time we lived there other than an occasional cold. God blessed us in so many ways, big and small.*

## Visiting Kostroma

Since officially leaving Kostroma in 2010, I have been back to visit twice. I returned in 2013 for the church's 20th anniversary. Then in 2015, Ginny and I went back for three weeks to attend the graduation ceremony at Light to the World Christian Academy and to meet with several different groups for teaching, encouragement and fellowship.

*Kostroma Christian Church's 20th anniversary*

One of the greatest areas of growth we witnessed during our last trip was the many young families in the church. Throughout the first ten years or so, there were just three or four complete families in the church. Most of the people were either children, college age youth, older adults, singles, or someone who came without their family. It was somewhat rare for us to see full families come to church together. Then, young people in our church married each other and started families. Then, they invited their friends who also came as a family. It is a great indication of a healthy future for the church.

I preached what may have been my last sermon in Russia during those three weeks. We recognize that we are at the age where the 30 hours of flight time, walking through terminals and Russian streets, stair climbing and bus riding, is simply too much for our bodies. We don't know if we will make it back again.

*Ilya Sheptunev & Ron Cook (2015)*

As we look back over 23 years of ministry, we praise God and revel in His grace that we could be part of this miraculous work. We can't wait to get to heaven where we can sit together and speak unhindered in the same language.

## The Mission Continues

Though we are no longer part of it, the mission to bring Russians to Christ in a truly Russian church continues. Kostroma Christian Church is meeting on Sundays. The students still meet on Saturday evenings. They serve God through many ministries in the church and out in the community, reaching people for

*Ginny Cook (front row, white shirt) with a
ladies' group at Kostroma Christian Church*

Christ. The Light to the World Christian Academy is
beyond successful. The church has good young leaders, a terrific worship team, an active youth group,
and great children's ministers. They serve the home-
less, single moms, children in the hospital, grieving
widows, and more.

An American who visited Kostroma on a mission trip, Connor Farris, later married a Russian girl
named Natasha. Connor majored in Intercultural
Studies at Ozark Christian College. He volunteers in
children's ministry and occasionally preaches on Sundays with his wife by his side interpreting the message.

One ministry in particular is cherished by those

in the church and community: My Way Camp. Every summer, the church puts together a Christian camp with worship services, games, swimming, and so on. They chop down trees to build fires, sleep in tents, and do team-building exercises. This is geared toward teenagers, but is open to basically anyone. It is a great ministry where people make decisions for Christ and grow in their faith.

*Children performing at a Christmas play*

*Conner & Natasha Farris*

*Teens leading worship at Kostroma Christian Church*

*Worship service at My Way Camp*

*My Way campers & counselors*

*Nadya & Sasha Zhurin*

# *Final Thoughts*

Over the years, many people have asked us how we could accomplish so much in such a short period of time, especially what we achieved in the first four years. I typically responded with this: "We set our eyes not on what is seen but on what is unseen, since what is seen is temporary and what is unseen is eternal" (2 Corinthians 4:18). This was exceptionally true in the summertime when we still had daylight most of the night. We didn't have a TV, radio, or newspapers (there was nothing offered in English). We had nothing else to do, so we worked all times of day preparing lessons and sermons, teaching and preaching, and training others to do the same. We had no other interests. We took no vacations. We just did what we felt the Lord sent us to do.

Not knowing the language had a lot of handicaps, but it also helped us follow through on God's plan for our work there. Moreover, I believe God supplied us with an extra measure of health and strength during our days in Russia.

God used so many people from both sides of the ocean and brought them together on this journey. That in itself meets the qualifications of the definition of "miracle" stated in the introduction. We can never say *spa-si-ba* (Russian for "thank you") enough to the hundreds of people who have been part of this ministry. I am so glad that God pursued Ginny and me to embark on this journey. I have been blessed beyond anything else in the first half a century of my life! I don't know what my life would be like without having this new life after 50 years old, but it would not be anything as great as it turned out.

Mission to Russia is continuing on the journey with the plan to multiply churches in Russia and other Russian-speaking nations. They hope to plant many more churches over the coming years. We pray God's blessing on them, that thousands more will come to know Christ as Savior through their ministry.

On the follow page you'll find a timeline showing key points in the ministry of Mission to Russia. It began with us in 1992, but it certainly doesn't end with us. As you've read our story, we pray that you would reflect and ask God, "How might I be involved in your Mission to Russia?"

To find out more about Mission to Russia, visit their website at Mission2Russia.org.

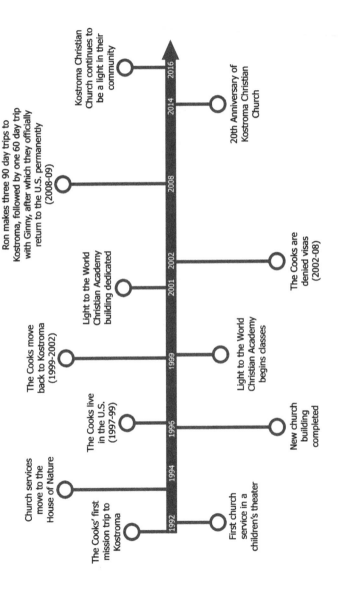

Church services move to the House of Nature

The Cooks' first mission trip to Kostroma

The Cooks live in the U.S. (1997-99)

The Cooks move back to Kostroma (1999-2002)

Light to the World Christian Academy building dedicated

Ron makes three 90 day trips to Kostroma, followed by one 60 day trip with Ginny, after which they officially return to the U.S. permanently (2008-09)

Kostroma Christian Church continues to be a light in their community

First church service in a children's theater

New church building completed

Light to the World Christian Academy begins classes

The Cooks are denied visas (2002-08)

20th Anniversary of Kostroma Christian Church

1992  1994  1996  1999  2001  2002  2008  2014  2016

# Personal Testimonies from Russia

THE FOLLOWING TESTIMONIES ARE EVIDENCE of the miracles that God brought about through our ministry in Kostroma, Russia. They are communicating in their own words so at times the wording may seem awkward, partly due to translation into English.

## INGA IVANOVA:

*There was this special time. When they came here I was interested in the Americans—to see them for the first time—I was very amazed by them. Maybe there are not many people of this type. I got interested in the service that took place in the theater. I had many questions about the service, and I came up to Ginny. There were so many people she wasn't able to clarify all the questions, to get the answers to all my questions. So when I parted with Ginny, there were tears in my eyes. She was crying too.*

*Then I wrote a letter to her in the U.S. I wrote her a desperate letter. I wanted to accept Jesus as my personal Savior, to come to understand God, but I had many doubts. I thought, while the Americans are here—OK—I believe in God and Jesus is in my heart, but what will happen when they leave— who will care about me? What will happen to me when they leave?*

*And once I came to know that Ginny and Ron Cook are coming to Kostroma—to live here to set up a Christian Church, I made up my mind to attend the church and I became a Christian and my life completely changed since then. Now I have joy and peace and comfort in my heart and life in spite of our difficult living situation in Russia.*

## ROMAN TYAZHEV:

*What kind of person was I before I accepted Christ? Why did I start believing in God? How did my life change? Well, before I came to the Lord I was a usual person. I did not have bad habits, I did not use curse words, I was not easygoing. I did not have any common interest with other young people. I did not read books. I was just a boring person.*

*But somewhere deep in my soul I was seeking for some-*

thing beautiful. I felt that in my soul there is some void, and I was looking for a thing to fill that void with. At the time, I did not think that only God could fill that void. Once when I was walking along empty corridors of the orphanage I thought about life, about my future, and I dreamed about happiness, beauty, and love. That very time God gave me a chance to get to know Him better.

I had an opportunity to go to the summer camp to rest. I refused to go at first, but I changed my mind after my classmates talked me into going. In the camp, I heard about God. The camp was held by American Christians, and they were busy in their work or telling about God. It was at this camp that the time came for my change of heart. They prayed for us to learn how to bring our problems to God with love.

I don't remember how and when it all happened, but to me it looked as if I was in some other place. I felt my heart was overflowing with joy, happiness, and love to God and to Jesus Christ. I felt the most beautiful and happiest moment in my life at the time. I was not by myself. God was with me. I felt His presence, His love to me and the rest of the world around.

I have been a Christian and go to church for six years. I believe in Jesus. I am so happy that God brought me close to Himself. In my best dreams I could not imagine that God has some plans for me. All blessings to you in Jesus, our Savior.

## ILYA SHEPTUNEV:

*My name is Ilya and I am 27. I was born and grew up in Kostroma, Russia. My childhood did not differ from the childhood of other children who live in our city. My parents are good people. They always treated me with love and took care of me.*

*For some reason I began to be set apart from my parents when I was a teenager. We did not have close family relationships. Our relationship was a riddle for me. They did not understand what was happening in my soul. Maybe it was that way because I was a self-dependent boy. From my early years I have been doing everything myself. I did my school studies by myself. You can say that the street brought me up.*

*Like many others, I started smoking for the first time at age seven. It was maybe then that I began having a secret life. At first the secret life made me feel special and distinguished me among the others. Before I turned 12 I tried to be either an athlete or a hooligan. When I was 12 I started drinking alcohol. I became a leader in trying to find money to buy beer, vodka, and wine—I did not care what I drank. Whenever I got drunk I had a feeling of bravery and joy that lasted for a while.*

*I spent my 6th and 7th grades more or less sober while in school. The gang I had assembled gathered on holidays in my family summer house (without my parents of course) to party and drink. When we did not have alcohol we just sucked some benzene (gas) out of the tank of a motor bike and sniffed its vapors.*

*Of course my parents noticed that something was wrong with me, but I was very cunning in hiding my addictions. When I was in the 8th and 9th grades I used different tranquilizers and I smoked marijuana regularly. I quit studying in school. I learned how to escape from bad grades and somehow passed my classes.*

*Constant lies and betrayal and stealing from my parents became my lifestyle. Added to all of this was the rock music culture with its idols and examples of rock starts. Kurt Cobain became my idol and influenced me for a long time. His philosophy of life brought an awful way of thinking into my life. Taking drugs became a normal way of life for me.*

*By the time I turned 15, I had become a drug addict. I did not have any plans for the future. I just lived thinking where to get money to smoke or drink. When I turned 16, I tried heroin intravenously and gradually my dose was increasing, and I understood that I could not live without an injection. By that time it was the way of my life, and it was turning into an ugly picture. All I saw of my life was a person sinking into a filthy, disgusting swamp, and the result of all was death.*

*Sometimes I had a desire to quit using drugs, and I had enough will power for two or three days and then I used the drugs again. By this time I had stolen all the jewelry and stuff from my parents, and I started stealing money from my older brother and forced weaker kids to give me their money. I borrowed money, but never gave it back. I helped those who had money to get on the needle. After I used heavy drugs during one year, I found out that I was infected with hepatitis B and C.*

*By this time my mother was a believer in the Kostroma Christian Church which Ron and Ginny Cook from the U.S. started. I remember that my father would try to keep my mother from going to the American church which he said was a sect and that she had been brainwashed there. I supported my father. She tried to tell me about God, but I did not want to listen to her. Usually it all ended with arguments and insults of my mom. But all that time (five years) she kept praying for me.*

*I know now that God began working with me in His special way, but it took a while.*

*I celebrated the new year night of 2000 at my friend's apartment. They all drank much. For some reason I did not want to drink. The dose of heroin I took seemed to be too weak for me, so by 1:00 a.m. I was sober. I was in a strange mood and I started thinking about my life. It seemed that I saw myself from another side. I spent the rest of that night alone sitting in the room. Now I understand that I was not alone—God was there. He came and found me, though I did not look for Him.*

*I had been crying for a long time. My heart was suffering. I understood that I had been living a worthless life. I felt ashamed for having hurt all the people that I had touched including my own family. I wanted to clean myself from all that, but all I could see was a dark void, and I was asking forgiveness of the one that I did not know and did not know where to find Him.*

*After that night I kept on using drugs but it did not bring me joy any more. A week later, hepatitis started to progress and it made me suffer greatly—so much that I could not eat. It was disgusting for me even to breath. Two days went by and I was taken to the hospital. It was at that time that all my relatives found out that I was a drug addict. My father threatened me a lot, but my mother came to the hospital every day and tried to comfort me and told me about God's love. I kept on doubting. I could still only think about where to get drugs. I spent a month at the hospital using drugs.*

*One Sunday, my mother came for a visit and we spoke about God again. I remember starting to cry at the moment of that talk. After she left, I went to my room and the other addicts suggested that we have a dose and for the first time I refused. The next day I left the hospital. I spent a week at home never wanting to leave. I knew that the same old things were out there waiting for me. The doctors had given me pain medication so I was not in pain.*

*On another Sunday my mother suggested we visit the church. I agreed because this was a place where I would not meet with my druggy friends. I also wanted to please my mother.*

*I liked it there! The church people surprised me. They were different from what I expected. Cheerful people met me. They welcomed me in such a way as was opposite of what I expected. I liked the church service and the singing and even the sermon although I understood little of it. I liked it when they read the Bible and prayed together.*

I spent the next week reading the Bible. Before opening it, I prayed to God and asked Him to help my understanding. I asked Jesus to forgive my sins and become my Lord and Savior. I asked Him to change my life. In a few days, I quit smoking and using bad words. I devoured the Bible, prayed regularly, and began to visit the church. In a few weeks I was baptized. The church became a kind of rehabilitation center for me. I attended all Sunday services and other services.

Every week day I went to the Bible college. In the day time, I went to the church to help build the Christian school. My life was changed. I began preaching the gospel to my friends, and some of them came to the church with me. Some time later, I met my future wife Julia. We fell in love, and next July we will celebrate our 8th anniversary. Three years ago God gave us a son, and we are expecting another child in March. It has been 10 years since I quit using drugs. Serving God and getting to know our Lord Jesus Christ better became the main service of my life.

## VERA TYUTRINA:

My "coming to the Lord" story began in 2004 when my daughter got seriously sick. Medicine did not help, and she could die. My daughter and I spent a whole month in the hospital. During one of my sleepless nights while crying in my pillow, I did the thing, which even a non-believer might do in a moment *of despair—I addressed to God praying for the recovery of my daughter. In that prayer, I promised God that if Polina (my daughter) got well, I will believe in the power of the Lord, and I will get baptized. The Lord heard my prayer and she was healed. But at that time, I did not keep my promise. So He, like the true father, began to wait for me patiently and then He just called me.*

*My former classmate and friend, Lena Koritova, phoned me and said that the school where she works needed a teacher. I began working in the Christian school Light to the World. It was in the school where I met true Christians and I realized that it was not just by chance that I came there. God had brought me to his house and reminded me of my promise.*

*Now, I am in the beginning of the true way. I go to the church on Sunday worship services and I go to women's group with pleasure. I have great desire to find out more about our Lord Jesus Christ and then tell our students about him as much as I can. I have found the church where I can do it.*

## SASHA ZHURIN:

*When I was a teenager I did not know God, and I was wandering like a blind man from person to person, from one sin to another trying to quench that pain of my soul, that loneliness and uselessness. I did everything that my friends suggested. I was ready to do anything just to feel important and wanted.*

*From the time when I was in 5th grade, I attended the Sambo Club (wrestling), but I did not do any wrestling. I had friends who attended the club and I began to run around with them. I began to cheat, curse, steal things from my parents. We all strayed from our parents, and we found older friends who taught us all the wrong things. We hated everybody including each other. We needed money to entertain ourselves so we stole things, robbed the drunks, broke into cars, and stole car radios. At night we bought alcohol, smoked herbs, sniffed benzine and glue. One day that all quit being a pleasure, I fell even deeper and started using heroin.*

*In March of 2000, there were three months left before my school graduation. It was time to make a decision about my future. At that time several events happened and plunged me into complete despair. First we robbed one of the shops, and I was caught by the police and had to go to prison for a short time. Secondly I found out that I was infected with hepatitis C. I can't begin to tell you about the atmosphere which reigned in my family when my parents found out that their son was a drug addict infected with hepatitis and would soon go to prison.*

*I made up my mind that I would soon take "a golden shot" (overdose on drugs) and die from this life. But it seems that God had something else for me that I knew nothing about. The next day one of my friends named Ilya left the hospital where he spent a whole month. He was being treated for hepatitis. I met him at school, and I could not recognize him. He did not use drugs any more, he did not smoke, did not curse. When*

*I questioned him about why he changed so unexpectedly, he began telling me about some god. Everybody in the grade took him as a schizophrenic. But the change that happened to him bothered me greatly, and I agreed to go together with him to some church which seemed strange to me.*

*I had never seen anything like this church before. I was amazed by the eyes of those believers. They shone with peace, happiness, and joy and were not on drugs. There was something real, sincere, pure in them. Their hospitality amazed me. These people were happy because I came to visit them!*

*The next day after school I went to my old gang's place of "fellowship," if you can take cursing, insults, despising each other, mockery, etc. as fellowship. We were all interested in one and the same question—where to get some money to buy a dose. I remember that I went home that day earlier than usual. I thought about what I saw at that church the day before and what I saw in my gang that day. That was the first time when I understood the difference between God and the devil so clearly. That evening my parents took me to the village where my granny lived. I was separated from my gang and the city life for the whole seven days. All I took with me was the New Testament which I was given at the church the day before.*

*I spent several days reading the Bible. I became scared. I was in despair, I was in slavery of sin, loneliness, uselessness— is there a way out? If there is a way out, it should be like it is described in the Bible. God created the earth, humans, and the universe. And humans are not just a mistake of nature. I was created by a loving Creator, and He did it on purpose. He did not do it just to hurt me and then enjoy watching me be tortured. No! He did it for me to live in peace with Him. After realizing it, I began to pray and I gave my life to God through repentance and baptism.*

*God set me free from my addiction. I love fellowshipping with God. I love fellowshipping with other believers. I met my wife at the church in the youth services. We studied at the Bible college together. This way I gained not only knowledge about God and Christian faith, but how to use my knowledge and gifts. I became the youth pastor at Kostroma Christian Church. My wife Nadya ministers as a Sunday school teacher and a worship team member.*

*Seven years have passed since my first prayer. I am alive. I was healed from my sickness. I take my recovery as God's miracle. There are people who need me. I have my family. My happiness and basis of my faith is my life with Christ. He loved me first.*

*God gave me hope and meaning for my life. Now I have a purpose—to glorify Christ. I know that there are many people who are reading my testimony now, and you love God and keep yourself pure before Him. We are connected in Christ. We are separated by time and distance, but we will have a whole eternity to get acquainted, to fellowship and glorify our God. Let's get ready for that meeting. Now let's say together: "Worthy is the Lamb to receive all power and wealth, and wisdom and strength, and honor and all blessings."*

## Angela Klyushkina:

*I have no parents of my own. My granny brought me up till I turned seven, and then I was sent to an orphanage. I graduated from high school and studied to be a kindergarten nurse.*

*I was married when I was 20. My husband was 11 years older than me. When I was 23 I gave birth to a son. He was born three months early and weighed a little over two pounds. He and I stayed a long time in the parental hospital. I was told in the birth room that my baby would not survive. I addressed to God even though at that time I was not a Christian. I knew nothing about God or Jesus or salvation.*

*My husband turned out to be addicted to alcohol. After seven years of marriage, I took my son and left my husband. I had to live in a dormitory for two months. During that time, I studied how to sew at a sewing club where I met Lena. She told me about how the kids at the church made crafts, etc. I thought that I should take my son there. Just because of my curiosity, I took my son and went to the church to have a look. I was amazed and surprised by the way church people welcomed me. They were so hospitable.*

*Shortly after that I accepted Christ as Savior and was baptized into him. Even though I still struggle with many problems I have gained true happiness.*

# Board Members

Many thanks to the following men and women who have faithfully served as Mission to Russia board members, both past and present:

| | |
|---|---|
| Ron & Ginny Cook | Tim Clark |
| John Cannon | Linda Bergner |
| Nita Sherrill | Chuck Schmidt |
| Alan Baumlein | Glenn Anderson |
| Randy Jones | Mike Pabarcus |
| Ken Peterson | Ryan Wells |
| Eddy Sanders | Dan Stoll |
| Dan Drake | Daryl & Carolyn Marshall |
| Mark & Sheryl Dennett | Jeff & Suzie Wollman |
| Dr. Carl & Kathy Meyer | Curt & Debi Eyman |

# Acknowledgements

WE ARE BURSTING WITH GRATITUDE for all God's saints who have been part of this ministry throughout the years. There are too many people to list by name, but we want to recognize some who stand out.

**A very special thanks goes to:**

Daryl and Carolyn Marshall, our forwarding agents from the very beginning.

Mark Dennett of Valley Center, Kansas who was our first and long-time banker and official caretaker of all the legalities needed for living in two countries. We also want to thank Mark's helpers and financial bookkeepers, Nita Sherrill and Linda Bergner.

Ron Lamp, Rod Harris, and Mark Richison: Illinois ministers who were our first short-term helpers. They stayed with us a month, did mission work, and provided us with funds to purchase a car so we wouldn't have to travel by city bus to carry all of our materials and equipment by hand to teach the Bible in the schools.

Emmanuel Christian Church, Stoneboro, PA, for bringing more than 20 people and all necessary materials for our first Vacation Bible School.

Tim Clark, pastor at Emmanuel Christian Church and the first long-time chairman of the Board of Directors of Mission to Russia.

John Cannon, pastor of Jerusalem Christian Church in Greenville, PA who was a long-time board member and made many ministry trips to Kostroma.

Curt and Debi Eyman, lay ministry workers who took off a year from their jobs to live in Russia and to work with our children's ministry.

Marshal and Cindy Smith from Scottsbluff, Nebraska, for spending six months in ministry with us.

Jena Thatcher, who spent more than a year ministering to the young adults in Kostroma.

The Dopps family, chiropractors from Wichita, KS, who gave money to have New Testaments printed in the Russian language. From their gifts, more than 70,000 New Testaments were printed.

Bud Yoder, for evangelism training at Kostroma

Christian Church. Bud spent three months at the church, living in a room in the church building.

The leadership at Valley Center Christian Church, who sent us to Russia and has sponsored the work financially to this day.

First Christian Church in Hugoton, KS, and Riverlawn Christian Church in Wichita, KS, for their sponsorship towards us from the very beginning.

There are literally hundreds of others who came on short-term mission trips and did ministry during these years. Thank you to all who have contributed to our efforts and God's plan in Russia.

# About the Authors

RON AND GINNY COOK have been married for 53 years. They met while attending Platte Valley Bible College, now called Summit Christian College, in Gering, Nebraska. They pastored several congregations over thirty years, before starting Mission to Russia. After serving with Mission to Russia for twenty years, the Cooks are now retired and living in Andover, Kansas.